Branch Lines to Horsted Keynes

Then and Now

An Ivatt 2-6-2T locomotive, No. 41318, makes a fine sight as it pulls away from Horsted Keynes in the spring sunshine on 16th April 1955. The train, the 4.3pm from Lewes to East Grinstead, is composed of two 3-sets. The set immediately behind the engine is a SE&CR 'Birdcage' rake, while the other coaches are of later, Southern Railway design. Apart from the loss of the tall starting signal and third rail this scene remains very much the same today. *C. Hogg*

Sheffield Park in 1955...

On 7th May 1955, a few weeks before the cessation of normal services on the Lewes to East Grinstead line, BR Standard Class 4MT 2-6-4T locomotive No. 80033 drifts into Sheffield Park station with the 5.18pm train from Brighton to Victoria. In those days the south end of the station had a spacious air, which is heightened in this view by the large amount of empty siding space. It is likely that the train would have halted for a few minutes to enable the locomotive to take on water, the supply being much more plentiful than at Horsted Keynes.   *D. Cullum*

... and in 1995 *(opposite)*

Almost forty years later the Bluebell Railway's SE&CR C Class 0-6-0 No. 592 was photographed at the same spot prior to working a train to Kingscote. This view today is considerably restricted by the sizeable locomotive shed on the left, and growth of trees on the opposite side of the line which almost hide the pumphouse. On the day this picture was taken the sidings were particularly congested by berthed rolling stock. The romantic image of a sleepy branch line station has been lost for ever at Sheffield Park, and today the station fulfils a new role as headquarters of one of Great Britain's leading preserved railways, which gives pleasure to thousands of visitors each year. But visitors who yearn for the atmosphere of the old days are still catered for, because the meticulously restored station at Kingscote epitomises the true rural branch line station. The contrast could not be more marked.   *J.G. Mallinson*

Branch Lines to Horsted Keynes

Then and Now

Michael S. Welch

Featuring Photography by John Goss and Graham Mallinson

© **Michael S. Welch and Runpast Publishing 1995**

Typeset by Viners Wood Associates, Painswick, Glos.
Printed by The Amadeus Press Ltd, Huddersfield.
ISBN 1 870754 33 6

CONTENTS

Plate Numbers

Lewes to Barcombe	1-30
Barcombe to Newick and Chailey	31-45
Newick and Chailey to Sheffield Park	46-76
Sheffield Park to Horsted Keynes	77-110
Ardingly Branch	111-124
Horsted Keynes to West Hoathly	125-163
West Hoathly to Kingscote	164-179
Kingscote to East Grinstead	180-202

On the bright spring morning of 16th April 1955, Fairburn Class 4MT 2-6-4T locomotive No. 42081 accelerates away from Newick and Chailey station with the 8.3am London Bridge to Brighton train. The train is formed of a Maunsell compartment coach, immediately behind the engine, and a Bulleid 3-set, which was one of a batch built by the Birmingham Railway Carriage and Wagon Company. The Fairburn tank locomotives were regular performers on the Lewes to East Grinstead line during the first half of the 1950s, but did not reappear when the line reopened in August 1956. The station and goods yard site were later sold for residential development, and there is now no trace that a railway ever existed here.

C. Hogg

INTRODUCTION

When I first visited the Bluebell line in June 1963, the line south of Sheffield Park as far as Culver Junction had already been abandoned, but at least the Ardingly branch was still functioning. North of Horsted Keynes the track was still *in situ*, but was disused. When the Ardingly branch closed four months later, BR decided to remove all the surplus track and the Bluebell soon found itself isolated from the BR system. Despite this handicap the Bluebell continued to flourish, and in the mid-1970s the first tentative steps were made towards restoring the route to East Grinstead. Twenty years later trains are running to Kingscote once again, and reopening to East Grinstead before the end of the century is a possibility.

This album, however, attempts to portray the many changes which have taken place on the Lewes to East Grinstead line and Ardingly branch since BR steam days. The majority of the archive pictures date from the 1950s, but a sprinkling of earlier pictures is also included. I have been very fortunate to obtain a large number of unpublished illustrations from many previously untapped sources, and I am grateful to all those enthusiasts who had the foresight to record everyday scenes on the lines before the preservation era. It is fair to say that without these pictures compilation of this book would have been impossible. It seems that the Bluebell was much more widely photographed, particularly in BR days, than I had ever imagined! Throughout the book I have endeavoured to produce a balanced selection of illustrations in order to show the principal features of the lines, but my choice of subjects has been largely dictated by the availability of archive photographs.

While researching for the album I paid many visits to the abandoned sections of the lines and found this aspect of compiling the book particularly rewarding. Despite the (almost) forty years which have elapsed since trains last ran south of Sheffield Park it was pleasing to see that so much of the course of the line is still so readily indentifiable. Most of the bridges are still standing, and in some cases are still used for their original purpose. Only at Lewes, and on the site of Newick and Chailey station, has development completely obliterated the old railway. It should be noted that the trackbed is private property, and readers wishing to explore the remains of the railway would be well advised to obtain permission in advance from the landowner.

Readers may be surprised that I have broken away from the traditional format of 'then and now' books which are usually evenly divided between the past and present scenes. This is principally due to the fact that many 'now' scenes on the abandoned sections of the line consist of repetitive views of bushes, trees and undergrowth and little else, and I felt that such scenes would be of limited interest. Sussex is generally considered to be the most heavily wooded county in Great Britain, and certainly nature lost no time in reclaiming some parts of the abandoned trackbed, which have become impenetrable jungle. Generally I have tried to use only 'now' pictures which contain at least some tangible evidence of the former railway's existence. The omission of some of the less interesting 'now' views has enabled more of the older photographs to be included, and I feel this greatly enhances the album. I hope you agree!

Finally, I would like to point out that the maps (which generally date from LB&SCR days) are intended to give a general impression only, and do not necessarily relate to the illustrations.

M.S.W. Burgess Hill, West Sussex. May 1995.

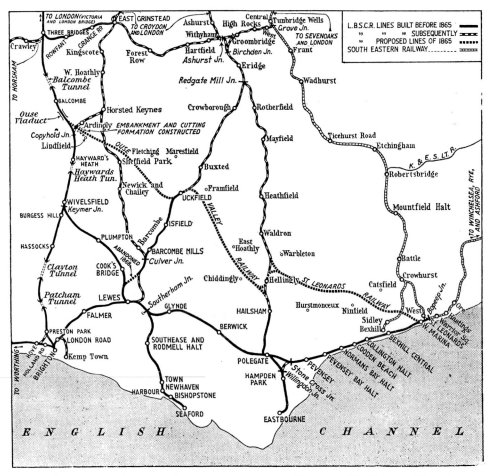

Railway map of eastern Sussex.

Courtesy, *The Railway Magazine*

1. Class D3 0-4-4T No. 32390 stands at platform 2 on the 'main line' side of Lewes station on 4th October 1953. The locomotive was working a railtour, organised by the Railway Correspondence and Travel Society, which traversed a number of branch lines in east Sussex. The train started at Three Bridges and ran directly to Eridge before traversing the 'Cuckoo Line' from there to Polegate. It is pictured here shortly after arrival from Polegate (via the Lewes goods lines) with the locomotive waiting to run-round before returning to Three Bridges via Sheffield Park. No. 32390 was the last survivor of its class, outliving its penultimate sister engine by almost two years. It was active right up to the end of its working life, being employed by Brighton shed on a variety of duties until withdrawal on 19th September 1955.
N.W. Sprinks

Few Sussex towns have a more fascinating and complex railway history than Lewes, which has had a total of five stations or halts within its boundaries. The first railway reached Lewes from Brighton and opened for business on 8th June 1846. The line ran into a terminal station at Friars Walk where an imposing building was built in classical style, with massive Corinthian pilasters. On 27th June 1846 the line was extended from Lewes to St Leonards, and just over a year later, on 2nd October 1847, the route from Keymer Junction opened. During 1847 two new through platforms, known as the Pinwell platforms, were constructed to the south of the terminus, and in theory these facilitated through running. Most trains, however, still used the terminus which involved time-consuming reversals: one of the most acutely inconvenient arrangements imaginable! To add to the confusion, a down platform was provided at Southover largely for the purpose of collecting tickets, though this was only open from 1845 to 1848.

The LB&SCR chairman described the original 1846 station as 'the most incomplete and injudicious station ever erected', and it became clear that action would have to be taken to revise the layout. Eventually, on 1st November 1857, a new station was provided west of the junction of the Brighton and Keymer Junction routes with platforms serving both the up and down lines. This eliminated many of the operating problems associated with the old layout. It should be noted that at this time the route from Uckfield was not yet completed but opened for traffic, using the Hamsey loop, on 11th October 1858. The route via Hamsey was short-lived however, and in 1868 a new stretch of line was brought into use enabling trains from Uckfield to approach Lewes from the east and to proceed direct to Brighton.

The 1857-built station was starting to prove inadequate however, and in order to increase the number of platforms and ease the radii of the curves it was decided to construct a new station a little to the south of its predecessor. This cut straight across from Southover Road to the east side of the town, and all tracks were slewed across to form a junction south and east of the 1857 station. In addition, the route of the Uckfield line was altered once again in order to facilitate through running to and from Brighton. The new station was brought into use on the 17th June 1889 and remains largely unaltered to the present day. It featured both up and down loops on the Brighton side platforms and a loop in the down direction only on the London platforms.

Perhaps one of the most interesting aspects of railway development at Lewes is the fact that so much of the original infrastructure survived until quite recently. This was largely because the goods facilities were adjacent to the original terminus building and not directly accessible from the new layout. The original Friars Walk station building survived until the 1960s when, regrettably, it was demolished.

Lewes

2. Despite the many years which separate the photographs there are few major differences between them, the most noticeable change being the loss of the signal gantries at the platform ends. Note that the platform numbers have all been altered, Nos. 2 and 3 in the previous picture now being Nos. 1 and 2 respectively. The mention of the comparatively new station at Moulsecoomb, in the Brighton suburbs, on the platform sign at least indicates that not all the changes that have taken place on BR have been for the worst. This picture was taken in December 1994.
John Goss

3. The rooftops of Lewes provide a distinctive backdrop to this delightful shot of the 9.30am East Grinstead train pulling out of Lewes station on a bright morning in October 1956. The train is running on a track which was served by platform faces on both sides, but sadly this interesting and unusual feature was later deemed to be superfluous to operating requirements. The track was removed and the space between the platforms subsequently filled in. The station itself is one of the finest in the south of England as befits the county town of East Sussex. This picture was taken during the period of the 'sulky service', when BR was forced to reintroduce services due to the discovery by a local resident that closure of the line contravened the original Act of Parliament authorising the railway. Services continued to operate for a further eighteen months until the legal situation was resolved.   *P. Hay*

4. The rooftops remain broadly the same and the attractive station buildings are also untouched by the passage of time. The estate agent's huge advertising hoarding has gone, however, and an equally obtrusive radio equipment room – complete with radio mast – has replaced it, neither of which do anything to enhance this end of the station. The platforms serving the former double-sided track are clearly visible. A twelve-coach e.m.u. formation, led by '4-BIG' (Class 422) unit No. 2209 is waiting to leave Platform No. 1 with a Victoria to Hastings train on 19th December 1994.   *John Goss*

5. A BR Standard 2-6-4T comes off the Uckfield line with a train from East Grinstead during the last few days of services, in March 1958. The train formations had been specially strengthened to accommodate passengers making a farewell trip on the line prior to closure, hence the use of a six-coach rake. The photograph is dominated by a massive area of downland which rises to a height of 538ft. above sea level. The electrified tracks on the right, beyond the signal box, lead to Eastbourne and Seaford.

G.Daniels

6. The splendid LB&SCR signal box and chalk downland are still visible from the east end of Lewes station, but virtually everything else has changed considerably. The course of the Uckfield line has been completely obliterated and mature trees now stand on the trackbed; they also conceal much of the downland which gives this end of the station a distinctive backdrop. Not surprisingly, the track layout has been rationalised and flat bottom rails have generally replaced bullhead track. The train, formed of preserved '2-BIL' unit No. 2090 leading '4-SUB' No. 4732, is the 4.4pm Seaford to Brighton, a timetabled working for which BR provided these 'heritage' e.m.u.s as part of the celebrations marking the 150th anniversary of the London to Brighton line. Since this picture was taken, on 24th August 1991, a footbridge has been built across the tracks beyond the signal box.

J.G. Mallinson

7. The 1.55pm Tunbridge Wells West to Brighton train, hauled by Class E1 4-4-0 No. 31507, rumbles across the girder bridge which carried the Uckfield route over the goods avoiding line at Lewes, on 11th February 1951. This rare view also reveals the complicated trackwork installed in the tightly-curved sidings, presumably to save space in the yard's restricted area. Two sets of 'three way' points are clearly visible and on close examination a third can just be discerned before the cattle pens in the middle of the picture. The stretch of downland in the background, Cliffe Hill, is one of the few features which remain unaltered today.   *J. J. Smith*

8. Apart from Cliffe Hill in the distance, there are few clues in this picture to suggest that it is the same location as the previous shot. The goods yard, and Uckfield line tracks above, have been obliterated without trace, yet in contrast a few yards behind the photographer, Lewes Station is almost untouched by the passage of time. The block of flats was built in the early 1990s.   *J.G. Mallinson*

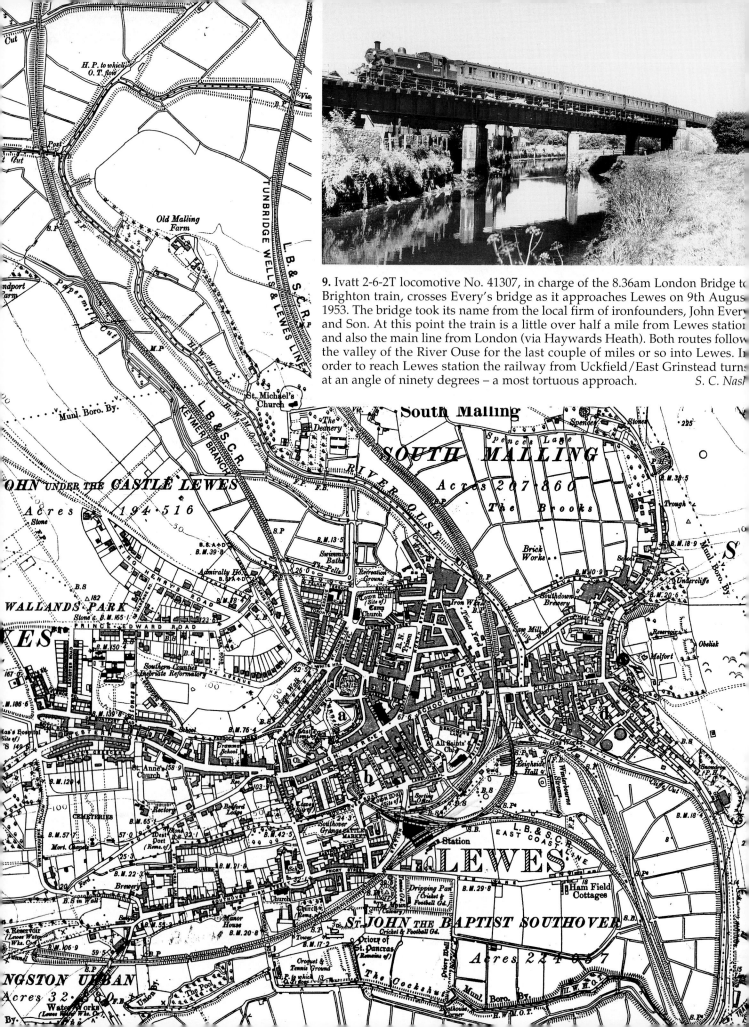

9. Ivatt 2-6-2T locomotive No. 41307, in charge of the 8.36am London Bridge to Brighton train, crosses Every's bridge as it approaches Lewes on 9th August 1953. The bridge took its name from the local firm of ironfounders, John Every and Son. At this point the train is a little over half a mile from Lewes station and also the main line from London (via Haywards Heath). Both routes follow the valley of the River Ouse for the last couple of miles or so into Lewes. In order to reach Lewes station the railway from Uckfield/East Grinstead turns at an angle of ninety degrees – a most tortuous approach.   *S. C. Nash*

10. After crossing the River Ouse the railway briefly heads in a north-westerly direction before entering a long, deep cutting near the village of South Malling. The line then begins to change direction, a long sweeping curve taking it round to the north-east. In this view BR Standard tank locomotive No. 80154 threads the cutting with a Lewes-bound train during the final weeks of the 'sulky service'.

G. Daniels

South Malling

11. Due to the profusion of young trees which have become established on the cutting sides this picture was taken from the trackbed, thus enabling the bridge to be seen. The trackbed is used by local residents as a footpath and is almost completely clear of bushes and trees. This scene, looking north towards Hamsey, was photographed on 26th March 1994.

J.G. Mallinson

12. Class C2X No. 32438, allocated to Brighton shed (75A), enters South Malling cutting hauling a southbound freight train in June 1956. This locomotive was originally constructed by Vulcan Foundry as a class C2 in 1893, but was rebuilt with a larger boiler in February 1924 and reclassified C2X. The second 'dome' on the boiler originally housed a top feed arrangement, but this was later discarded although the 'dome' was left on the boiler top. No. 32438 was withdrawn from service in December 1961 and subsequently scrapped. Sadly, no engines of this type survived into preservation. The train is passing beneath the bridge seen in the background of the previous illustration. *P. Hay*

The Lewes to East Grinstead line was only on the tail end of a number of schemes which were proposed during the fierce rivalry which existed between various companies during the mid-nineteenth century. If some of the earlier plans had materialised it is possible that the line would never have been built and the railway map of the area would have appeared completely different. One of the earliest schemes – first mooted in 1835 – involved a line through East Grinstead and West Hoathly to Lindfield and on southwards through Wivelsfield. This was one of a number of suggested routes from London to Brighton, but was ruled out due to the high construction costs involved. The following year another idea was put forward: this suggested linking Seaford and London via Chailey North Common, Lindfield and Hoathley Hill to connect with the proposed South Eastern line at either Godstone or Oxted. However this proposal was not pursued because during the same year Rennie's route from the Capital to Brighton via Balcombe was given assent by Parliament, and formed the principal route of the LB&SCR which opened in 1841.

Despite the arrival of the railway in Brighton other concerns still wanted a slice of the traffic to the fashionable and rapidly expanding Sussex resort. In 1863 a prospectus sponsored by the Chatham and South Eastern companies extolled the advantages of their 'Brighton Line'. This was planned to run from Beckenham to East Grinstead, Newick and Lewes to a terminus at Kemp Town. Two years later the same combination promoted the Surrey and Sussex Junction Railway from Croydon to Groombridge through the vicinity of East Grinstead.

At this point the LB&SCR decided to reinforce their territorial advantage with the construction of a number of new routes, including the Uckfield line, which helped to head off competition for its lucrative Brighton traffic. A threat to Eastbourne remained however, and in order to combat this the Ouse Valley Railway was sanctioned in 1864. This was routed from the famous Ouse Viaduct, just north of Haywards Heath, to run via Lindfield, Sheffield Park, Uckfield and Hailsham. Contractors were already at work when the failure of the famous banking house of Overend and Gurney in 1866 put an end to the railway mania born of that period. For a further sixteen years the East Grinstead – Haywards Heath – Uckfield triangle was destined to remain empty on the railway map. In 1876 the South Eastern Railway proposed the 'Metropolitan and Brighton Railway' which was planned to run from Beckenham to Godstone and on to Brighton via East Grinstead and West Hoathly using an identical route to that originally proposed in 1835. This was fiercely opposed, as might be expected, by the LB&SCR, and also local gentry in the locality south of East Grinstead, who were suspected to have plans of their own. The proposal was eventually rejected.

At this time there was considerable dissatisfaction with the general standard of service provided by the LB&SCR. In 1875 the 'North Sussex Gazette', based at East Grinstead, reported with an optimistic air about developments in the town but was not apparently impressed by anything connected with the Three Bridges – Tunbridge Wells railway. 'We regret that we cannot speak well of railway matters', reported the paper, adopting a serious tone. The paper accused the LB&SCR of neglecting the requirements of the town, despite a substantial increase in traffic of all kinds, and cited unpunctual passenger trains and poor connections at Three Bridges and Tunbridge Wells as a particular source of complaint. The station precincts at East Grinstead were also criticised for being poorly lit, this being a cause of accidents.

Ten years previously a pressure group, chaired by Viscount Pevensey, then the future Earl of Sheffield, had been formed to oppose the LB&SCR's Ouse Valley Line and backed a rival 'London, Lewes and Brighton' proposal, but the financial crisis at that time put paid to these developments. The people who comprised this group, mostly local gentry and prominent citizens from the Lewes and East Grinstead areas, agreed to gather together once again to promote a completely independent railway linking Lewes and East Grinstead with London.

Its proposed title was the Lewes, East Grinstead and London Railway and it was the intention to construct three sections – north and south of East Grinstead and a short branch from Horsted Keynes to Copyhold Farm. The latter was, of course, the Ardingly branch which linked up with the Brighton main line. There was a degree of support for the proposal in both Lewes and East Grinstead because it was seen that a direct connection would benefit both towns and certainly represent an improvement over the existing rail services which involved a change of trains. A contemporary correspondent thought the venture was 'a landowner's line, with possibly somebody behind them'. It can be reasonably assumed that the 'somebody' was Henry North Holroyd, Third Earl of Sheffield. Certainly, all the indications were that he was the driving force behind the scheme.

On Saturday, 30th September 1876 the provisional committee of the Lewes, East Grinstead and London Railway met at the Star Hotel, Lewes, with the Earl of Sheffield in the chair. The purpose of the meeting was to discuss the question of applying to Parliament for the necessary powers to construct a railway between the two Sussex towns and the Capital. Those present included William Lanham Christie, the Member of Parliament for Lewes, and prominent citizens from Lewes, Newick and Chailey. Also present was John Wolfe Barry who was to be the line's engineer. The committee received his report favourably and instructed him to proceed at once with a survey. It was agreed that a Parliamentary Bill should be prepared and the necessary plans drawn up. Two firms of solicitors – appropriately one from Lewes and another from East Grinstead – were appointed to deal with the long haul of legal matters which lay ahead. In addition an executive committee, chaired by the Earl of Sheffield, was appointed.

During the ensuing months the scheme was progressed by the committee and various meetings held at places as far apart as London and Brighton. During this period they approved the ruling gradient for the line, which had been recommended by the line's engineer, and opened a bank account. During their fourth meeting, held on 6th January 1877, the committee felt that the able chairmanship of the Earl of Sheffield should be formally acknowledged and a vote of thanks to him was proposed and recorded. Perhaps the committee members also had their financial state of affairs in the back of their minds, because it was becoming clear that they were failing to attract the necessary funds and were relying to a large degree on the Earl's generosity. Further meetings of the committee took place, but it was clear that it was not going to achieve its objective without substantial outside assistance. Approaches were made to the LB&SCR, and following a meeting at London Bridge Station in 1878 two LB&SCR directors appeared on the board of the Lewes and East Grinstead Railway (L&EGR). The original proposal to construct a line north of East Grinstead was dropped, also plans for double track south of Horsted Keynes.

The LB&SCR later built its own line north of East Grinstead. The L&EGR gradually faded from the scene and although the company was still in existence when the route was opened it was clear it existed only in name and very little would have been achieved without the LB&SCR. Despite the fact that the L&EGR failed to realise its objective it can be fairly said that without its initiative and enterprise in the first place the line would probably not have been constructed, and the first meeting at Lewes in September 1876 was when it all began.

13. An unidentified Class C2X approaches Hamsey church bridge with a train from East Grinstead in October 1956. At this point the line is elevated above the flood plain of the River Ouse, which is on the right of the photograph. The bridge on the extreme left of the picture carried the railway across a man-made cut. Note the primitive conditions on the footplate of the locomotive – the crew are using a storm sheet as protection while running tender-first.

P. Hay

Hamsey

14. The course of the line is still clearly visible at this point, and is likely to remain so for many years due to the substantial nature of the earthworks. The bridge across the cut has been removed, though, and scrub is gaining a hold on the sides of the embankment. Beyond the site of the bridge, the trackbed is hidden from view by a number of trees which have sprung up since this section of line closed in early 1969. This picture was taken in August 1994.

J.G. Mallinson

15. From Lewes to Culver Junction, East Grinstead and Uckfield line trains shared the same double track line. At Culver Junction, seen here, the single track of the Bluebell line diverged to the left leaving the route to Uckfield to carry straight on to Barcombe Mills station which is just out of sight about half a mile away. In this view, photographed on 14th May 1951, a commendably clean Class I3 4-4-2T No. 32026 has just negotiated the sharply-curved junction layout while working the 3.35pm Oxted to Brighton train. The substantial girder plate bridge carried nothing more than a farm track over the line. The locomotive, one of a class of twenty-seven distinctive Atlantic tanks, first saw the light of day at Brighton Works in March 1909 and it is recorded that building costs amounted to £2,982! Apart from one wartime casualty, the entire class was taken out of use in the early 1950s, this particular example being withdrawn three months after this picture was taken.

J.J. Smith

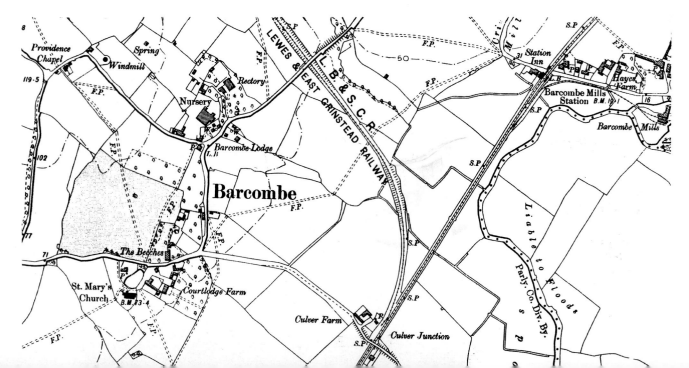

16. The fireman of Class C2X No. 32438 collects the staff from the Culver Junction signalman on an August day in 1956, shortly after the reintroduction of services. Note the wooden walkway provided for the signalman to enable such operations to be completed safely. Part of the signal box is just visible on the left of the photograph.   *P. Hay*

Culver Junction

17. Oh dear, what a transformation! Apart from the substantial girder plate bridge and a concrete fogman's hut (which is just out of view on the left-hand side) nothing of railway interest remains at this isolated location, seen here on 20th March 1994. The double track formation is now traversed by farm tractors, while the bridge provides a degree of protection for the storage of pallets and other miscellaneous agricultural equipment.

J.G. Mallinson

18. The unusual track layout of Culver Junction is depicted in this view taken in March 1958, a few days prior to the cessation of services on the East Grinstead route. Note the sand-drag on the left of the picture; this was presumably provided to safeguard the main line in the event of a runaway on the branch which climbs away on a 1 in 80 gradient. The main building of Barcombe Mills station can just be discerned in the distance, behind the signal post.
E. Wilmshurst

19. A view of the rarely-photographed signal box at Culver Junction. The nameboard is privately preserved by an enthusiast in Hove.
P. Hay

20. The neat haystacks and barn at Culver Farm provide a delightful rural setting for this portrait of C2X Class 0-6-0 No. 32438 climbing away from Culver Junction in August 1956.
P. Hay

21. Some of a small flock of inquisitive sheep keep a wary eye on the photographer as he endeavours to find the location from where the previous picture was taken, which was not a straightforward task. A mound of earth now marks the course of the railway. The sheep are obviously intent on maintaining it in tidy condition and appear to be succeeding admirably! In the background, the line of the Uckfield route can just be discerned, while part of the bridge near the site of the former Culver Junction is also visible in this March 1994 picture. The South Downs west of Glyndebourne provide the backdrop.
J.G. Mallinson

22. A few hundred yards further north of the previous location an East Grinstead to Lewes train was photographed a quarter of a mile from Culver Junction. It has just passed beneath a bridge which carries the lane connecting the villages of Barcombe and Barcombe Cross. No. 80154 was the final steam locomotive constructed at Brighton works and it achieved a particular claim to fame when it hauled the last Bluebell line trains on 16th March 1958. In view of this it was earmarked for preservation in the early days of the Bluebell Railway, but when No. 80154 was withdrawn from service the Bluebell were struggling to raise money to purchase the freehold of their line and were forced to forego their opportunity to purchase the engine, which was subsequently scrapped. In recent years sister locomotive No. 80064 has operated on the Bluebell on temporary loan, while another example, No. 80100, owned by a group of Bluebell members, is a long term restoration project.

J.H.W. Kent

23. The trackbed is still in reasonable condition at this point, although trees are encroaching. Beyond the bridge there is a mass of impenetrable undergrowth, however, making a walk towards Barcombe station impossible. Note the shed in the adjacent garden which appears to be in good condition after at least thirty-eight years of use! *Author*

24. Barcombe was a typical country station serving a small rural community. In this delightful view, looking down the station approach from the main road, the station's quiet position is plain to see: there is not another building in sight! The ancient oil lamp on the roadway and enamel station sign with its noticeboard are prominent. The posters advertise the cheap day excursion tickets available to South Coast resorts and also London, Croydon and, rather strangely, Clapham Junction. Perhaps the last mentioned destination was aimed at the train spotting fraternity! The vintage scene is somewhat spoilt by the ugly fenceposts which do not 'harmonise' with their surroundings in any way. This photograph was taken on 31st August 1954.
J.H. Aston

Barcombe

Barcombe was by far the smallest station on the line. Its modest facilities comprised of a single platform with a signal box at the north end, and a tiny goods yard of two short sidings which were connected to the running line by a goods loop. The latter was installed in 1905 – hitherto northbound goods trains were shunted by means of a wire tow rope. Barcombe was never used as a crossing point for passenger trains. Despite being the poor relation of the other stations in terms of facilities, Barcombe was nevertheless provided with a substantial station building which was similar to others on the line.

Fortunately some of the early history of Barcombe station and details of the day-to-day routine of running the station have survived and make fascinating reading. One of the earliest 'eye-witness' accounts came from the late Mrs. Sarah Funnell who was a guest at the official opening of the Bluebell line in August 1960. She recalled the harsh winter of 1880/81, when repeated snow falls during January cut off outlying cottages and farmhouses, causing complete isolation and in extreme circumstances, starvation. The third week of January had been particularly severe with especially heavy falls of snow and bitterly cold nights.

The desperate plight of the local folk was relieved by the navvies whose work building the Lewes to East Grinstead line had been temporarily halted by the bad weather. They were summoned out of their shanty town by the rough voice of their foreman and set to work with their picks and shovels clearing the compacted snow and ice from the local lanes, and indeed the streets of the village itself.

Mrs. Funnell's father was the village blacksmith and he was busy all day sharpening blunted tools. The building of the line caused an upsurge of trade generally at the smithy. By the middle of 1881 the track-bed had been levelled with the contractor's little trolley wagons running to and fro. The station building was also beginning to take shape. At the turn of the century the

Station Master, who lived in the station house, was responsible for attending every train, seven days a week. He earned the princely sum of thirty-two shillings per week and had only one day off a month, when a relief was provided. When on duty he would wear a very smart frock-coat with two pockets behind and loops of black silk on each sleeve. He also wore a peaked cap with an elaborate brass plate which featured the quartered arms of London, Brighton, Portsmouth and Hastings. His day's work was long and hard, beginning with despatching the first train at 7.17am and seeing off the last train of the day at 8.0pm during the winter months, or 9.40pm in the summer. In addition to his usual platform duties he had to spend a lot of time working on the accounts of the substantial quantity of milk traffic forwarded from the station. It was once said that passengers could sometimes hardly get on to the platform because of the number of milk churns strewn around! All cash received in connection with the milk trade was kept in a leather bag and stored overnight in a safe in the station house. It was usually despatched on the first morning train, being placed in a special safe box in the guard's brake van.

At the time the LB&SCR rigidly enforced a £1 fine on Station Masters who failed to observe the regulations regarding the handling of cash. The railway company's auditors generally visited the station once every three months to check that all was in order. During the period from 1912 to 1926 both stations serving Barcombe village were placed under the supervision of the Station Master at Barcombe and a bicycle was provided by the LB&SCR to enable him to visit Barcombe Mills station as frequently as he chose. During 1926 the arrangements were altered with responsibility for Barcombe Mills being transferred away, Barcombe and Newick and Chailey coming under the jurisdiction of a Station Master based at Sheffield Park. This arrangement survived until the end.

25. The former Barcombe station, now a private residence, is all but hidden from view by a line of tall trees which also screen the back garden. This is bordered by a wooden paling fence which has replaced the wire fence formerly in use. The station approach is now a private road, providing access to the former station house, and also to several new dwellings which have been built north of the station. The gardens of these properties appear to cover the old trackbed. This scene was recorded in March, 1994.
J.G. Mallinson

26. In the late afternoon sunshine of 3rd July 1954, Fairburn 2-6-4T locomotive No. 42105 awaits departure from Barcombe with the 4.18pm London Bridge to Brighton train. Between Culver Junction and Horsted Keynes the formation was constructed for double track, but the route between these points was always single track except for passing loops at Newick & Chailey and Sheffield Park.

D. Cullum

27. The 4.28pm East Grinstead to Lewes train, powered by BR Standard Class 4MT tank locomotive No. 80011, passes the deserted former station at Barcombe on 8th September 1957. The bare station nameboard and tufts of grass gaining a hold on the platform surface underline the sad air of decay and dereliction. *C. Hogg*

8. The two previous illustrations were taken from the roadbridge immediately south of the station, a lofty viewpoint which provided a splendid panorama of the station and surrounding countryside. The same cannot be said of the bridge today, however, because during the intervening years tall trees have become established on the site, and are rapidly obscuring the view. It is likely that within a few years the station building will be completely hidden, doubtless much to the relief of the occupants, whose back garden will no longer be visible to inquisitive passers-by on the highway. The trackbed has been filled in to provide a sizeable lawn area, and, except for the loss of the canopy, the station building is intact and in a respectable condition.   *J.G. Mallinson*

In March 1937 Mr. R.J. White, who started his railway career at Norbury, south London in October 1928, moved to Barcombe as a Grade One Porter. His recollections of daily life at the station highlighted the friendly atmosphere, where it seems most of the passengers were known by their first names! He lived in a council-owned cottage during his stay at Barcombe, the station house already being occupied by his colleague Cecil Long and his family. When Mr. White's fiancee came to visit she lodged in the station house with the Long family. Mr. White recalls that his cottage was lit by oil lamps: primitive days indeed! When there were parcels to be delivered in outlying areas a local carrier would usually be employed. He would call at the station about twice a week, with his horse and cart, looking for trade.

At this time there was still regular goods traffic at Barcombe, and our informant recalls that the daily pick-up goods train would sometimes stop to attach or detach privately owned coal wagons for the local merchant, Mr. Richards. Occasionally during the winter an empty wagon would be left for loading of sugar beet. When the goods train arrived it was essential that it was shunted quickly because no other train movements could take place between Culver Junction and Newick. On Sundays, the porter at Barcombe worked a split shift of two hours in the morning (9am to 11am) and two hours in the evening (6pm to 8pm) and for this received remuneration of six shillings and four pence. During the summer there were additional duties rostered, assisting the porter/signalman at Barcombe Mills. These involved collecting tickets and operating the level crossing gates. An enhanced rate of pay was given for these duties, amounting to nine shillings and sixpence. Life at Barcombe station in those days seems to have been so friendly and relaxed. There are amusing tales of an entrepreneurial ganger, Phil Knight, who set snares to catch rabbits and sold them for one shilling a pair to train crews or any passengers who might be interested. Sometimes the staff would need to get from one station to another, but did not always take the train. A walk between Barcombe and Newick and Chailey took them past a stream where they could pick watercress to supplement their tea!

Following closure in 1955, Barcombe was one of the stations which was never reopened. The loss of their station was keenly felt by the villagers, particularly when the 'sulky service' was introduced in August 1956 and trains passed through without stopping. 'Please, please stop at Barcombe' was chalked on a wall at the station, but the request was ignored by the railway authorities, much to the frustration of local people. Following final withdrawal of services the line was lifted during 1960, and during August of that year a bulldozer was seen at work scraping ballast from the trackbed, as if it was attempting to remove all trace that a railway ever existed. Fortunately that was not realised and the station building, approach road and bridge survived. In 1989 the station house, described as a 'carefully converted piece of history' was offered for sale for £299,000. The current owners wish to retain the building's character and it will hopefully remain a tangible reminder of the railway's existence at Barcombe for many years to come.

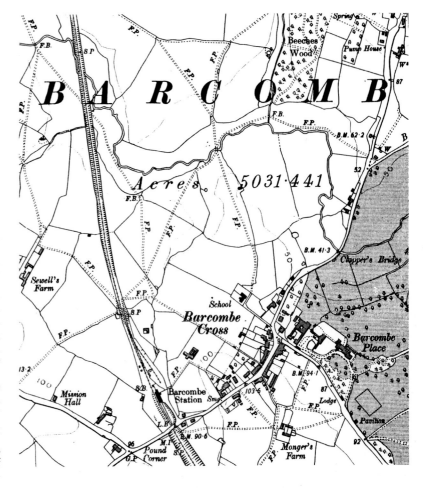

29. One of the saddest sights for a railway lover is that of a railway line being lifted following closure, as seen here at Barcombe on 28th February 1960. By this time the line had been closed for almost two years and nature already appears to be taking over. *G. Daniels*

30. When the author visited the site in December 1994 (with the landowner's permission) the structure of the bridge appeared to be deteriorating to the extent that BR, which is responsible for maintenance, have been obliged to install a framework of steel girders to support it. A similar installation made of timber, seen to the right, proved unsuccessful and had to be abandoned. Presumably the bridge will have to be replaced at some time in the future or, more likely, the old railway will be infilled and a short section of new road built on top. Whatever the solution, it appears that the cost will probably have to be borne by the long-suffering taxpayer. *Author*

31. The Class I1X 4-4-2T locomotives were attractive enough when running chimney first, but when working bunker first... well, perhaps the less said the better. Few locomotives look good when viewed from the rear and, at least in the author's view, these must surely be counted amongst the worst. The author was, however, delighted to unearth this shot of an I1X at work on the line. There were twenty of these machines and No. 2002, seen here leaving Barcombe with a northbound train on 14th May 1951, was the last one in service being withdrawn two months after this picture was taken. This particular locomotive spent much time in store at Eastbourne and Bognor Regis during the twilight of its career and this probably explains why its Southern Railway livery survived to the end. The building on the left of the picture is not the station house, as might be supposed, but a private residence. *J.J. Smith*

32. A footpath used to cross the line a few yards south of here and is still well-trodden today. Closure of the line provided the opportunity for the creation of another – unofficial – path branching off the existing one, along the trackbed. This is seen here, on 15th October 1994. On the extreme right-hand side of the picture can be seen the supporting poles for overhead power lines which follow the course of the old railway for much of the way northwards to Sheffield Park. A number of small bridges survive immediately to the north of this spot, offering a more tangible reminder of the line's course. *J.G. Mallinson*

33. On 25th May 1955 the 5.18pm Brighton-Victoria approaches Brickyard Farm, north of Barcombe, behind highly unusual motive power in the shape of former L&SWR Class T9 4-4-0 No. 30718. The elegant T9 was diagrammed specially to move the locomotive back to its home shed at Nine Elms. Note the rear vehicle, Pullman car *Savona*, which was also on its way home, in this case from Preston Park shops to Stewarts Lane depot. Many odd vehicles were sent on this train, including loaded horse boxes *en route* to destinations on the LMR and ER, for cross-London transfer by van train at Victoria. A nicely turned-out Maunsell three-set completes the train. Note the 1 in 75 gradient which applies at this point, as the train climbs away from the Ouse Valley towards the Weald. *S.C. Nash*

34. Today, it is impossible to stand at exactly the same spot as in the previous photograph due to the mass of undergrowth which continues to grow virtually unchecked. The course of the old railway is still unmistakable, however, principally due to its continued use as a footpath, which doubtless prevents nature from taking over completely. Knowlands Wood, in the background, appears to have expanded a little during the intervening period. There is a bridge across the trackbed at this spot which, amazingly, still retains the familiar soot marks generated by 75 years of passing steam trains, offering positive proof that these once passed beneath. This picture was taken in March, 1994. *J.G. Mallinson*

35. On the first day of the restored service, 7th August 1956, Class K 2-6-0 No. 32342 hauls a two-coach Lewes to East Grinstead train, approximately halfway between Barcombe and Newick & Chailey stations. The three-arch bridge just visible in the background carries a track which connects Oldpark Wood, on the east side of the railway, to the Newick-Cooksbridge road, on the west side. Note the passengers leaning from the windows, doubtless enjoying the unprecedented experience of travelling over a line which had just 'come back from the dead'.
G. Siviour

36. The course of the line northwards from Culver Junction is largely well-defined until just beyond this location, the second overbridge north of Barcombe, where sections have been bought by landowners. A prolonged spell of wet weather prior to the author's visit had turned the former trackbed into a quagmire. Note the overhead power lines.
Author

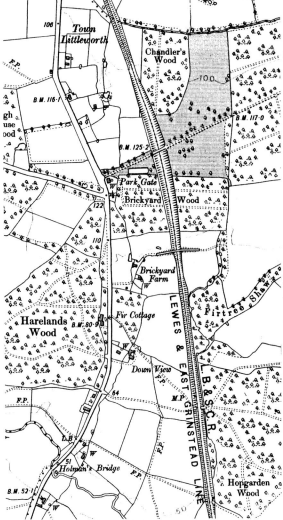

37. LB&SCR Class H2 Atlantic No. 32426, *St.Alban's Head* is seen powering a RCTS railtour on 14th August 1955. This train was originally planned to run on 12th June but had to be postponed due to a national rail strike. Note the bowler-hatted locomotive inspector on the footplate. The train, which includes a Pullman car in its formation, was photographed about a mile and a half south of Newick and Chailey.

S.C. Nash

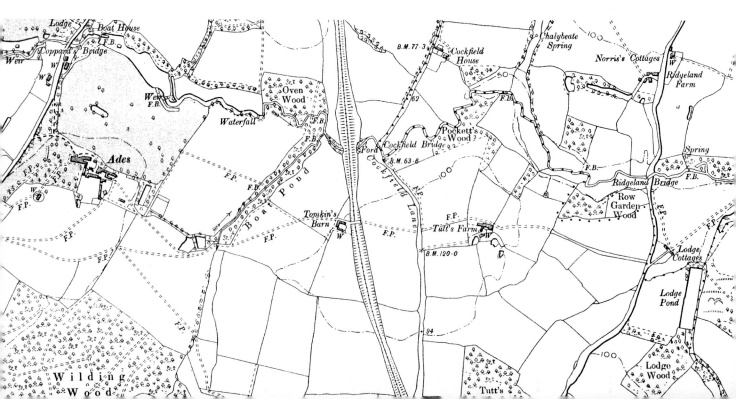

38. This picture, taken on 24th September 1951, shows the 3.35pm Oxted to Brighton train heading away from Cinder Hill tunnel, which is just out of sight in the distance. The train is hauled by an immaculate BR Standard 2-6-4T locomotive, No. 80016, which is probably being run-in following construction at Brighton works. Unfortunately for the passengers, though, their accommodation is decidedly dated, comprising a SE&CR 'Birdcage' set probably built before the First World War! Unlike many of its sister engines which were allocated to depots on other regions, No. 80016 was destined to spend all its short working life on the Southern, based at a variety of depots.
S.C. Nash

39. Despite the thirty-seven years which (at the time of writing) have elapsed since closure, the trackbed is still largely well defined, and a small bridge which carried the railway across a farm track is still extant, out of the shot, immediately behind the photographer. To the north, however, where the line entered a cutting at the approach to Cinder Hill tunnel, the course of the route is hidden by trees and dense undergrowth. The area in the immediate foreground is now part of a farm and used for grazing purposes. This picture was taken in December 1994.
Author

40. On Sunday 24th April 1955, Class C2X No. 32440 spent the day with the engineer's tunnel gantry train engaged in the examination of Lywood, Sharpthorne, East Grinstead Nos. 1 and 2 and Cinder Hill tunnels. It is seen here in the afternoon sunshine shortly after leaving Cinder Hill tunnel, presumably *en route* for Brighton at the end of a busy day. The photographer was obviously party to 'inside information' regarding this working which enabled him to obtain this very rare shot.

J.J. Smith

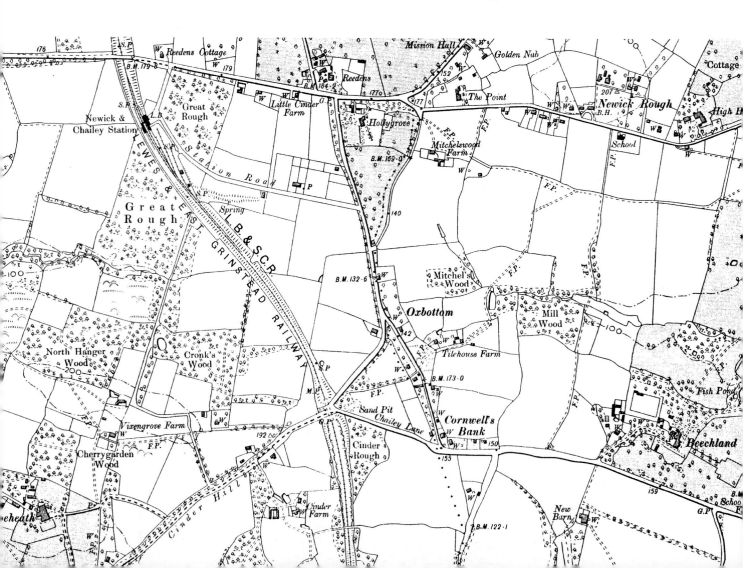

41. A Class C2X locomotive, No. 32528, is seen emerging from Cinder Hill tunnel with the 3.0pm East Grinstead to Lewes train in tow on 24th September 1951. Cinder Hill tunnel, situated about a quarter of a mile south of Newick and Chailey station, is the least pretentious of the three tunnels built for the Lewes and East Grinstead Railway. It is a modest affair, being sixty-one yards in length and lacking a brick face to the portals. But it had its moment of glory during the Second World War when, in 1942, the 1.20pm Brighton-Oxted push and pull train came under attack by an enemy aircraft. Fortunately, the driver was able to accelerate into the tunnel, where there was just room for his train to take refuge. *S.C. Nash*

Cinder Hill Tunnel

42. Cinder Hill tunnel is probably the most interesting piece of infrastructure still in existence on the closed section of line south of Sheffield Park, apart from Barcombe station. It is hardly worthy of the name 'tunnel', and was probably one of the shortest on the BR system. Records reveal that a change of gradient occurred inside the tunnel, the climb against northbound trains moderating from 1 in 75 to 1 in 115. The latter applied as far as Newick and Chailey station, where a level section was reached. Today the southern portal is completely overgrown, as seen here on 12th March 1994, but the northern entrance is relatively easily accessible provided great care is taken. Inside the tunnel indentations are clearly visible in the earth where the ballast was scraped away by the contractors dismantling the line. *J.G. Mallinson*

43. Class E4 0-6-2T No. 32504 pauses at Newick and Chailey station with a southbound train in February 1957. This picture was taken from the disused northbound platform: note the rusty up line which had not seen regular use for many years. Close examination of the photograph reveals a 'way out' sign indicating that passengers leaving the station did so at ground level, perhaps through the rear of the goods yard. Presumably the usual exit, to the station approach road via the staircase, was not used during the period of 'sulky service' running, due to the station being unstaffed.

P.S. Leavens

Newick and Chailey

44. When this scene at Newick and Chailey was recorded on 29th April 1956 the station had been closed for almost a year, but re-opened to passengers four months later. Note that all the rail surfaces are rusty. The road just visible on the right is Station Road (nowadays Lower Station Road), while on the left a wooden fence marks the boundary of the railway's property. Everything of railway interest in this picture has since been obliterated.

J.J. Smith

45. The ornate entrance porch is a striking feature of the station frontage of Newick and Chailey in this photograph which was taken on 26th March 1955. Note also the decorative chimney stacks and hanging tiles. *D. Cullum*

In 1903, with barely twenty years of public traffic to its name, the Lewes to East Grinstead line still bore a remarkably modern appearance and contemporary travellers remained lavish in their praises of the line. 'The station buildings', wrote one, 'are especially worthy of note for their elegance in appearance and the amount of accommodation they secure to the customers and servants of the Company. They are similar in style, but superior in size and finish', he went on, 'to those on the contemporary Chichester - Midhurst and Tunbridge Wells - Eastbourne lines'. The stations were undoubtedly most impressive, particularly East Grinstead with its 'two-decker' station, but of the smaller stations on the line Newick and Chailey was perhaps the most interesting, if only because it was unique.

The station was sited in a cutting south of the Haywards Heath to Uckfield main road which crossed the railway on a three-arch bridge. Because of the difficult location, a three-storey building was constructed with the basement at platform level and passenger facilities, facing the forecourt, on the middle floor. The staff living quarters were on the top floor. Amazingly, the building incorporated a refreshment room, the only one between Horsted Keynes and Lewes, and this served the local community as much as rail travellers, there being no

equivalent amenity in the immediate locality. The buffet had a very short existence, being closed in 1913. Its closure was a bitter blow(!) to the station staff who had almost a mile to walk to the nearest hostelry, the 'Kings Head' at Chailey.

Newick and Chailey handled a fair amount of goods traffic, particularly milk. The principal intake was farm machinery, coal, groceries and road-building materials. In addition to milk the main outgoing goods consisted of market garden produce, timber and fruit. One interesting facet of operations was a special morning train which started from Newick and conveyed schoolchildren to Lewes. There was a corresponding return working in the afternoon.

The refreshment room was the first amenity to be abandoned. In the 1930s the up platform buildings and footbridge were removed, while after the Second World War the station ceased to be a crossing point. During the final years prior to closure Newick and Chailey was a shadow of the original station, the loss of the up platform buildings giving it an unbalanced appearance. Following demolition a housing development sprang up and perhaps some of the residents are unaware that they are living on the site of a splendid country station.

46. Several piles of track panels litter the station and yard at Newick in early 1960. The track nearest the camera was the main running line, the other track being a headshunt which gave access to the goods yard. Note the piles of coal and sacks, on the right. Despite the apparent chaos all around it appears that the local coal merchant was still in business! Newick and Chailey station was almost entirely surrounded by mature trees, a most appealing and peaceful setting which was only disturbed by the rumble of traffic on the nearby Haywards Heath to Uckfield road. Following removal of the track, the station building remained *in situ*, but was a target for local vandals and became increasingly dilapidated as time went on. It was eventually demolished in July 1967.   *P. Hay*

In late 1959 BR decided to remove the track between Culver Junction and the roadbridge just south of Sheffield Park station. The job was put out to tender and the firm of Pittrail Ltd. were awarded the contract. In January 1960 they established a base in the former goods yard of Newick and Chailey station, which had reasonable road access. The task of removing the track panels was undertaken by a four-man team who used a rail-mounted crane. The panels were then transported to Newick and Chailey on bogie flat wagons to await

dismantling prior to road removal. Eighty years earlier hundreds of navvies had toiled away for almost four years to construct the line, but the small group of scrapmen took only four months to clear away the disposable assets of the single line section, the work being completed by Easter 1960.

Note: The illustrations dealing with the demolition of the line are not in journey order.

47. The demolition contractors employed a small Avonside diesel locomotive, *Kimberley*, to move track materials from the site of the work to Newick and Chailey station yard. It is seen here apparently stabled on the single line between Newick and Sheffield Park stations during the spring of 1960. *P. Hay*

48. The crane depicted here appears to be rail-mounted, so it seems rather strange that it is standing on top of the embankment and not on the track! Perhaps the contractors had another crane with which they could re-rail it, or maybe they used jacks. The location is half a mile south of Sheffield Park station; the line has just started to curve round towards the south-west before passing beneath the Chailey to Fletching roadbridge. *P. Hay*

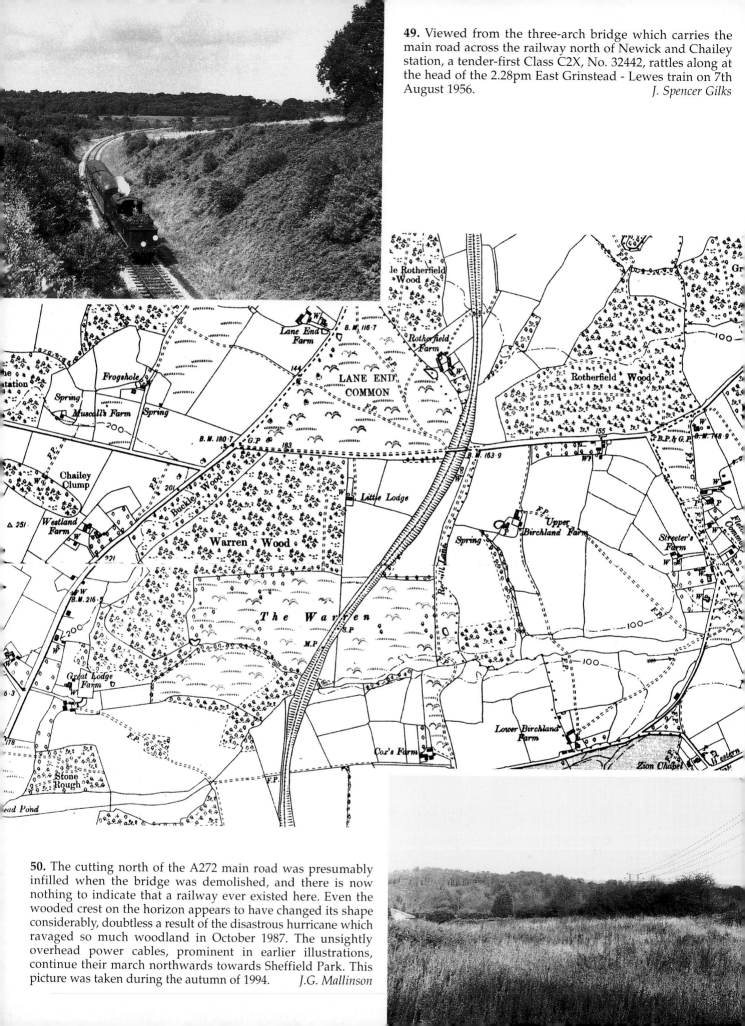

49. Viewed from the three-arch bridge which carries the main road across the railway north of Newick and Chailey station, a tender-first Class C2X, No. 32442, rattles along at the head of the 2.28pm East Grinstead - Lewes train on 7th August 1956.

J. Spencer Gilks

50. The cutting north of the A272 main road was presumably infilled when the bridge was demolished, and there is now nothing to indicate that a railway ever existed here. Even the wooded crest on the horizon appears to have changed its shape considerably, doubtless a result of the disastrous hurricane which ravaged so much woodland in October 1987. The unsightly overhead power cables, prominent in earlier illustrations, continue their march northwards towards Sheffield Park. This picture was taken during the autumn of 1994.

J.G. Mallinson

51. A view of the line on its last day of operation, looking north at a point about a mile north of Newick station. The tightly-curved nature of the line at this location will be noted. The conical-shaped conifer tree can also be seen in the following picture, thus providing an interesting reference point. *J. Scrace*

52. Maunsell-designed Class U1 2-6-0 No. 31900 is about to pass beneath the three-arch roadbridge near Fletching Common on 16th April 1955. The train is the 11.2am Brighton - Victoria which is formed of a Bulleid three-set, No. 799, with a Maunsell side-corridor vehicle on the rear. This location is just over a mile south of Sheffield Park station. *S.C. Nash*

53. Class C2X No. 32539 makes a very pleasant sight as it steams southwards beneath the bridge, also on the bright spring day o[f] 16th April 1955. It was powering the 12.28pm East Grinstead to Lewes train, which is understood to have been a Saturday footbal[l] excursion presumably run for the benefit of those attending a match at the Goldstone Ground, Hove. The provision of such a[n] unlikely working on this rural line may seem strange, but in those days private car ownership was not as common as it is toda[y] and public transport was more widely used. This train was not unique: similar trains ran on other Saturdays during this period[.] The coaches returned to East Grinstead attached to the rear of the 4.3pm from Lewes.
S.C. Nas[h]

54. During the years that have elapsed since the line was closed, trees have grown on the cutting sides at such a rapid rate that the course of the old line is in danger of being completely engulfed. The trackbed is still passable and used principally by horseriders, presumably from a local farm or stable. Note the ivy which covers much of the bridge.
J.G. Mallinson

55. Looking north from the same bridge towards Sheffield Park, the 3.35pm Oxted to Brighton train can be seen steaming along in the distance. Motive power is provided by Fairburn 2-6-4T locomotive No. 42080 and the date is 26th March 1955. This section is now so heavily overgrown that it is impossible to obtain a corresponding shot of the scene today, the view from the bridge being totally obscured by trees. *D. Cullum*

56. Class E4 0-6-2T No. 32467 puts on a pleasing smoke effect as it hauls a train for Lewes just south of Sheffield Park in early March 1958. The train in this picture is at the same spot as that in the previous photograph, although the camera positions are somewhat different! Note the fogsignalman's hut at Sheffield Park up distant signal, which by this time had lost its arm. Perhaps both items survive today, but are inaccessible due to the undergrowth. *P.S. Leavens*

57. This is the only picture the author has discovered of the bridge across the A275 road immediately south of Sheffield Park station. It is, therefore, of considerable historical interest which more than justifies its inclusion in this album.

Bluebell Archives

Sheffield Park

58. Virtually nothing remains of the bridge, apart from a small section of the abutments on the Sheffield Park station side. Note the private road to Woodgate Farms Dairy which leads off on the right of the picture. This photograph was taken in January 1995, which was a month of constant downpours, hence the flood on the road. The Autopoint No. 121 bus is providing one of the three services which, at the time of writing, operate from Lewes to Sheffield Park and return on Saturdays, proving that public transport to Sheffield Park station by road is not totally a thing of the past!

J.G. Mallinson

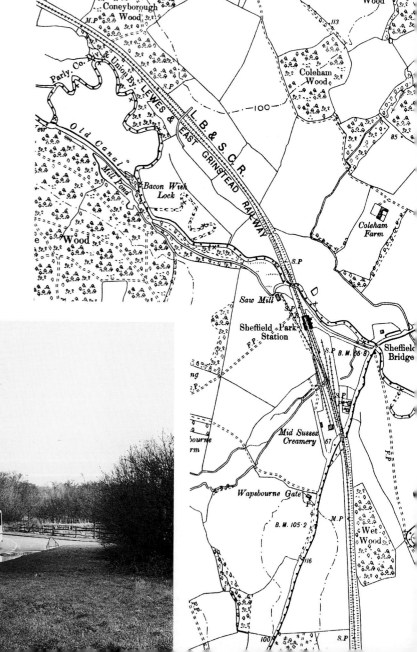

59. The bridge is seen again, this time from track level: two volunteers are at work on the left of the picture. Note that the recently erected buffer stops have a barrier of earth behind them, presumably to prevent a runaway vehicle falling into the road. This was obviously thought to be a danger once the bridge had been removed. A marquee, just visible in the middle of the picture, and large crowds on the down platform indicate that a special event was in progress. In fact, this picture was taken on 7th August 1960, the Bluebell's opening day. *J.J. Smith*

60. Most of the photographers who visited the Bluebell Line prior to closure took pictures at Sheffield Park station, and consequently shots of the station area are plentiful. But this view, looking south from the pumphouse siding towards the roadbridge, is most uncommon and therefore of special interest. Note the wagon in the goods yard on the left and stack of timber just beyond. Nearer the camera is a pile of coal, or possibly coke, judging by the small size of the pieces. The roadbridge carries two separate tracks across the highway, the main running line and also the shunting neck, the buffer stop of which is almost concealed by a telegraph pole. The train, hauled by E4 Class No. 32517, is the 4.3pm *ex*-Lewes, and the photograph was taken on 16th April 1955. *C. Hogg*

61. Sheffield Park station and goods yard present a sad sight in early March 1958. An unsuspecting visitor could have been forgiven for thinking the station was totally closed and awaiting the demolition men. Closer inspection would have revealed that one track was still in use, however, even if the remainder had a thick layer of rust.

P.S. Leavens

62. Seven and a half years later, on 7th September 1965, a similar aspect reveals a considerable transformation. The pumphouse, station and cattle pens are still there, but almost everything else has altered almost beyond recognition – even the loading gauge, which presumably was involved in an accident at some stage during the intervening period! The main running lines have obviously been treated with weed-killer but vegetation seems to be gaining a firm hold on the other tracks. The diminutive locomotive on the right is *Fenchurch*, which arrived by rail via Ardingly the previous summer, while the LB&SCR directors' saloon occupies the cattle dock siding.

J. Scrace

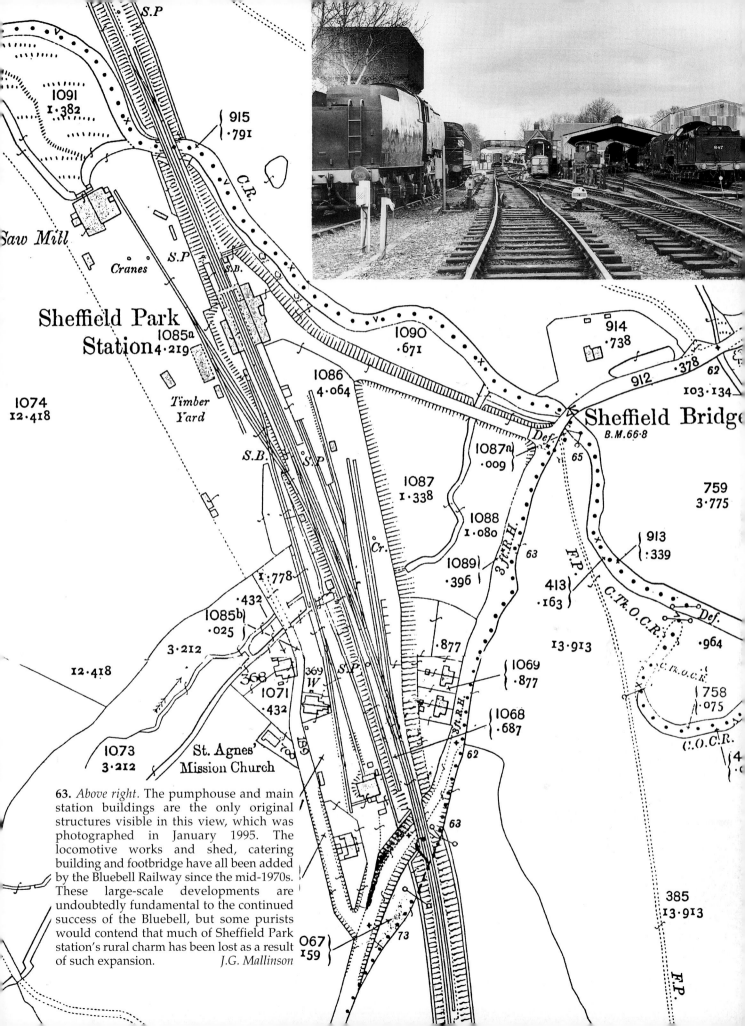

S.P

1091
I·382

915
·791

C.R.

Saw Mill

Cranes

S.P

S.B.

Sheffield Park
Station 4·219

1085ª

1074
12·418

Timber
Yard

1090
·671

914
·738

1086
4·064

912   ·378   62
103·134

Sheffield Bridge

S.B.   S.P

Def.

B.M.66·8

1087ª
·009

65

1087
1·338

759
3·775

1088
1·080

Cr.

I·778

·432

1089
·396

3·R.H.

63

913
·339

1085b
·025

413
·163

F.P.

C.Tk.O.C.R.

3·212

·877

13·913

·964

12·418

1069
·877

C.Tk.O.C.R.

368   369
W   S.P

1071
·432

1068
·687

758
·075

C.O.C.R.

1073
3·212

St. Agnes'
Mission Church

3·R.H.

62

63. *Above right*. The pumphouse and main
station buildings are the only original
structures visible in this view, which was
photographed in January 1995. The
locomotive works and shed, catering
building and footbridge have all been added
by the Bluebell Railway since the mid-1970s.
These large-scale developments are
undoubtedly fundamental to the continued
success of the Bluebell, but some purists
would contend that much of Sheffield Park
station's rural charm has been lost as a result
of such expansion.   *J.G. Mallinson*

067
159

73

385
13·913

F.P.

64. This view of the south end of Sheffield Park station, photographed in the early days of the preservation society, is thought to have been taken in the spring of 1961. The sole item of rolling stock on view is LB&SCR 'Terrier' 0-6-0T No. 55, *Stepney*, which had been restored during the previous winter. The newly-built asbestos-clad engine shed is on the left, whilst prominent on the right is the water tank and pumphouse. These were pioneering days when the whole concept of standard gauge railway preservation was completely new. At the time many people doubted whether the Bluebell venture would succeed, but they had not anticipated the strong public interest the line would attract, nor realised that its position close to large population centres and south coast holiday resorts would be crucial factors in its success. *Bluebell Archives*

65. Taken from a slightly different angle to the previous picture, this view shows the south end of Sheffield Park station in late 1981. Twenty years of progress and development have totally transformed the scene from that of an embryonic preserved railway with few assets to a world-famous tourist attraction. The first major change at Sheffield Park occurred in early 1975 when the first phase of the locomotive works was constructed, followed a year later by the giftshop on the down platform. This purpose-built shop replaced the former Hassocks station bookstall which found a new home at Horsted Keynes. The new engine shed, alongside the works, followed later, but the original shed was retained to house locomotives awaiting repair and is visible in the top of the photograph. Unfortunately the ornate pumphouse is almost totally concealed by foliage. The revised track layout incorporating the short-lived scissors crossover will be noted. *Bluebell Archives*

66. A later photograph, taken in early 1989, shows the scissors crossover in the course of removal while a new siding is being laid out on the left to provide accommodation for the Pullman train. The locomotives on view include no fewer than three in BR livery. No. 34023, *Blackmore Vale,* is on shed, out of service awaiting overhaul, while BR Standard 2-6-4T No. 80064 is standing at the top of the shed yard. Across in the pumphouse siding sits *Fenchurch* temporarily repainted as No. 32636. No. 80064 arrived on loan from an independent group based at the (former) Dart Valley Railway, Buckfastleigh, in the summer of 1984, but returned to the West Country in 1992.
Mike Esau

etching and Newick (for Piltdown)' was the clumsy and uninspiring me once proposed for Sheffield Park station which thankfully failed find favour with the authorities. The LB&SCR decided to call the ation 'Fletching' and this name actually appeared for a short time on ems such as platform oil lamps, signalmen's hand-lamps, and leather sh bags. The name bestowed by the Brighton Company infuriated the ewes and East Grinstead Railway board who insisted that the station ould be known as 'Sheffield Bridges', a proposal which had the crucial cking of Lord Sheffield. The audit office quickly produced a host of spatch bags marked 'Sheffield Bridges', but they were too hasty cause Lord Sheffield changed his mind in favour of 'Sheffield Park', hich resulted in the LB&SCR coming down in favour of 'Fletching and effield Park'. His Lordship was not amused by this decision and wrote the LB&SCR board asking them to reconsider. Eventually at their eeting of 13th December 1882 the LB&SCR Board of Directors agreed at the latter name would be abbreviated to plain 'Sheffield Park' in cordance with Lord Sheffield's wishes.

Sheffield Park Station is situated 6 miles 30 chains from the former lver Junction on a brief section of level track bounded to the north by short 1 in 160 grade towards Ketches Bridge and a mile of 1 in 82 uthbound gradient which commences half way along the station yard. e station is located at a point which is officially 42½ miles from ndon.

The close proximity of Sheffield Park with its spectacular pageantry eant that its function differed from that of the other stations on the line hich merely served the needs of the local people. The LB&SCR idently decided that many of the people attending events in the Park ould expect higher standards than the everyday traveller, especially

those coming down from London for the day who could be faced with a considerable wait for a return train. Consequently the washing and lavatory fittings were on a very elaborate scale with huge brass taps and oak panelling. A glass roof and ventilation slats enhanced the very pleasing effect.

Another distinctive feature of Sheffield Park in days gone by was its two signal boxes, named *North* and *South* which as their names imply, were located at each end of the station. This arrangement was simplified in the mid-1930s when both boxes were abolished in favour of a signal frame on the southbound platform which could be operated by a single porter/signalman.

A further peculiarity at Sheffield Park was the water supplies. In the early days the station had no running water at all, and this vital commodity had to be brought up in churns from Barcombe. Later the railway authorities entered into an arrangement with the adjacent Mid-Sussex Dairy Co. for the supply of water for the station house, which was collected at 9.0am each morning. Running water is thought to have been provided by about 1920, but this could not be used for drinking purposes without being boiled.

Passing steam locomotives were, however, much better provided for. Water supplies at Sheffield Park were pumped directly from the River Ouse and reckoned to be better for steaming compared with the more chalky water further south. Many drivers therefore preferred to stop there to take water if at all possible. This had other advantages for the crews because the water tank was often teeming with fish pumped up from the river and enthusiastic enginemen are reported to have made good catches!

67. A timeless scene at the south end of Sheffield Park station on a June day in 1954. An Ivatt Class 2MT 2-6-2T locomotive No. 41307, takes water before departure with the 3.35pm Oxted to Brighton train. This was one of a class of 130 engines constructed to an LM&SR design for light passenger and branch line work. No. 41307 was built at Crewe in 1952 and only had a short working life before being withdrawn from service in March 1966. The 4.3pm Lewes to Horsted Keynes train, headed by Class C2X No. 32536, is also taking water, in the up platform, before setting off on the last stage of its short journey. Both trains are formed of SE&CR 'Birdcage' stock.
P. Ha

68. In complete contrast to the previous view, crowds throng the end of the down platform at Sheffield Park after the arrival of an afternoon train from Horsted Keynes on 21st April 1962. *Bluebell* is on the front of the train while another small engine, doubtless sister locomotive *Primrose*, is at the rear. At that time the original B signalling arrangements were still in operation and trains to Horsted Keynes could only depart from the up platform. The train is, therefore, about to leave the southbound platform and pass over a set of points which will enable it to reverse into the northbound platform. The former down starting signal is already 'off' to enable the move to proceed. Note that *Stepney* is standing in the northbound platform before double-heading the next train with *Primrose*.
P.J. Lync

69. More than forty-one years later, in January 1995, the view from the same spot is dominated by the catering complex and footbridge, the principal station building being almost totally hidden from view by the latter. The water crane, and shunt signal are still in their original positions and provide a tenuous link with the past. Sadly, the tranquil atmosphere of this rural branch line station has gone, but mercifully it still survives at Kingscote! The coaches on the right formerly ran in the 'Royal Scotsman' and 'Queen of Scots' touring trains and provide luxury overnight accommodation for both visitors and volunteers. They were acquired in early 1992 on a five-year loan from Hunter International.

J.G. Mallinson

the early 1960s Mrs. Amy Barford, daughter of Mr. C.D. Skinner, a [for]mer stationmaster, gave this delightful first-hand account of [ev]eryday life at Sheffield Park. Her recollections relate to a summer's [m]orning just prior to the formation of the Southern Railway in 1923.

'We were aroused very early by the birds who were joined at [4].45am by the noise of the Mid-Sussex Dairy milk trolley. Seventeen-[ga]llon churns were being unloaded and taken across the line for the [d]own train (7.4am) together with one churn of cream which went [da]ily through to Brighton and another destined for Eastbourne. There [w]ould also be some milk for the up side to London. At 7 o'clock [M]essrs. Turner and Sons sawmills commenced work and their hooter [co]uld be heard for miles around. Their foreman, Mr. Blogg, would [be] crossing the line to the booking offce to collect his mail.'

This was 'rush hour' because two trains crossed at this time each [m]orning on weekdays. The up working had the locked cash box in [th]e guard's brake van and each stationmaster had to personally place [a] small leather bag containing cash received the previous day into [th]e box. These were later collected at London Bridge and taken to [th]e Treasurer's Department. The other leather bag, which had a brass [pl]ate stamped 'Fletching', contained accounts and general [co]rrespondence. This travelled loose in the van and was collected by [m]essengers who awaited the train's arrival at London Bridge. [N]umerous parcels for all the surrounding areas were usually [un]loaded off the up train. One regular caller at the station was a Mr. [Ba]nnister, the grocer at Nutley, who was one of the carriers and each [da]y came to the station to collect parcels and goods items for many [of] the landowners in his area. A sealed mailbag was also conveyed [on] this train from the postmaster at Lewes; the station clerk would [so]rt out the letters and hand them to the local postman. The [st]ationmaster also doubled as postmaster, selling stamps, postal [or]ders and suchlike. He also despatched parcels, both by post and [ra]il, so this must have placed him in a tricky position when customers [as]ked which undertaking was likely to provide the better service! It [is] recorded that Messrs. Turner and Sons bought their insurance [st]amps from him each month and presumably he carried out similar

business with other local concerns. The letter box outside the station entrance was emptied twice-daily and the contents despatched in a sealed mailbag on either the 1.54pm or 6.8pm trains to Lewes. It was on the latter train that newspapers arrived for Danehill and Fletching, while copies of the Brighton 'Evening Argus' were conveyed on the 5.8pm train from there to Victoria.

The summer morning routine, however, continued with the arrival of some local farmers, who presumably did not receive deliveries due to their remote location. The next surge of passengers would usually occur prior to the departure of the 8.35am London train which was very popular with those wishing to visit the Capital for a shopping expedition, or whatever. Most normally returned on the 4.10pm from London Bridge. Following this early morning period of comparatively frenetic activity, the stationmaster and his family would have breakfast, bacon and eggs cooked on two paraffin stoves. Life at the station house may have been leisurely, but it was certainly not without difficulties. The station's isolated position, some distance from the nearest village meant that there was no electricity and oil lamps had to be used for lighting, while log fires provided much of the heating. The occupants largely depended on deliveries for provisions; the milkman called at 8.30am every morning, also bringing meat from the butcher at Fletching. A baker from Scaynes Hill visited the station thrice weekly, while the grocer from Fletching made a weekly call.

In the evening the family provided their own entertainment. Mother played the piano, father sang, while a hand-wound gramophone was ready to take over when inspiration flagged. Summer Saturdays would see them active at the Sheffield Arms Tennis Club, which also arranged away matches at other local venues. Sundays were normally reserved for church-going. The curate at Chailey would cycle across every Sunday to hold a service at St.Agnes church, a 'tin' building adjacent to the timberyard. Congregations were sometimes so small that he would decline to hold a service. The monthly whist drives, held in the same building, were better supported especially during the winter months.

70. A train for East Grinstead pauses at Sheffield Park during the period of token service running. Motive power is provided by Class C2X No. 32434 of Brighton shed. Note the rusty up loop line nearest the camera.

S.C. Nash

71. During the months following closure Sheffield Park station became increasingly dilapidated. Stripped of its enamel station nameboard and with weeds covering the platform surface and running lines it looks a pathetic sight. Note that the signalling frame has been removed from the platform.

J.G. Mallinson

72. New building developments at Sheffield Park have been largely confined to the south end of the station where land was available, and happily the north end remains basically unchanged. Apart from the addition of a few enamel advertisement signs, and the unrestricted growth of a massive tree behind the station sign, the station area looks much the same as it did forty years ago. The concrete sleepers on the up line have gone, however, and can now be found on Freshfield bank, where they replaced a section of wooden-sleepered track which was in deteriorating condition. In this view a group of visitors can be seen admiring the SE&CR C Class locomotive No. 592, which is awaiting departure with a northbound train in January 1995.   *J.G. Mallinson*

73. Originally there were two signal boxes at Sheffield Park, but in the mid-1930s they were replaced by an open signal frame on the down platform as an economy measure. When the Bluebell commenced operations the hapless signalmen became a target for inquisitive children who were fascinated by the constant ringing of bells and pulling of levers. This was obviously a hazard to the safe operation of the railway and a decision was taken to totally enclose the frame, the work being undertaken during the winter of 1961/2.   *M.J. Mason*

74. During BR steam days many photographs were taken of southbound trains waiting to leave Sheffield Park station's dow
platform, but relatively few of northbound workings have come to light, especially those which show the sawmill. Here a LM&SR
designed 2-6-2T tank locomotive is seen pulling away from the station on a dull day, 21st May 1955, with the 4.3pm Lewes t
Horsted Keynes train. Once again SE&CR stock forms the train, and also that in the adjacent platform.   *G. Daniel*

75. It is interesting to see tha
while far-reaching changes hav
been taking place at Sheffield Par
station over the years, th
adjoining woodyard has als
undergone quite a visual trans
formation! On Bluebell propert
the most noticeable alteration i
the construction of the viewing
area on the right of th
photograph. This facility wa
completed in April 1993. It will b
noted that trains can leave fron
either platform, whereas in BI
days there was no such flexibilit
J.G. Mallinso

76. In beautiful low autumn sunshine *Bluebell* and *Primrose* enter Sheffield Park station with a train from Horsted Keynes on 29th October 1961. The L&SWR Adams 4-4-2T No. 488 and *Stepney* bring up the rear. This was a momentous day in the Bluebell Railway's history, being the first occasion on which through running into Horsted Keynes station was permitted by BR. *G. Daniels*

Sheffield Park station took its name from the nearby estate and in view of the Third Earl of Sheffield's close involvement with the promotion and construction of the line perhaps a few lines about the Earl and his estate would be appropriate at this point. The Third Earl of Sheffield was born as Henry North Holroyd in St. Marylebone, London, on 18th January 1832. His father was by any standard a wealthy man, owning over four thousand acres of land in Sussex, and other estates in Yorkshire and Ireland. The young man was given the courtesy title Viscount Pevensey and received a nobleman's education at Eton between the years 1844 and 1848. There he became a close friend of HRH The Prince of Wales, an association which continued into later life. He served in the army in India and also in the diplomatic service, but later returned home to enter politics, serving as Conservative MP for East Sussex. In 1876, following the death of his father, he took up residence at his country seat at Sheffield Park.

During his army service Lord Sheffield had developed great affection for the military and became one of their most enthusiastic patrons. He encouraged the volunteer movement, often allowing the soldiers the virtual freedom of his estate. On occasions mock battles were staged in the grounds and military revues arranged. The revues brought a boost in trade to local businesses, particularly publicans and an open invitation was invariably extended to local folk which ensured the Earl's popularity with his tenants and inhabitants of the surrounding area. The climax to these events was often a spectacular fireworks display. One remarkable result of the Earl's military connections was the display of an armoured train, apparently on a special siding (constructed beyond the roadbridge south of the station) which entered the grounds of Sheffield Park. Senior officials from the War Office are understood to have journeyed to Sussex to witness the huge cannon in action. That must have put the fireworks in the shade somewhat!

Another of the Earl's great interests was cricket. He became a member of the M.C.C. in 1855, but failed to gain distinction as a player. Cricket had, however, been played at Sheffield Park since 1846 and when the Earl moved there in 1876 it was natural that he would wish to develop the facilities. This he did to great effect with the result that the visiting Australian touring teams regularly played their opening fixture at Sheffield Park against an England XI raised by the Earl himself. The first South African team which came to

England in 1894 also opened their tour at Sheffield Park. Perhaps the most memorable occasion occurred two years later when the Prince of Wales (later King Edward VII) was present for the match against the Australians. In addition to maintaining one of the finest grounds in the Kingdom the Earl of Sheffield was also a generous benefactor to the Sussex County Club of which he was president for many years. He was also in the vanguard of Test cricket, taking an England team to Australia at his own expense in 1891-92. Towards the end of his life the Earl was generally regarded as an amiable gentleman. In society he was a member of the Carlton Club and associated with the Royal Historical Society, but when at Sheffield Park tended to live the life of a recluse. He avoided contact with members of his staff, preferring to issue instructions in writing. His staff were kept busy ensuring these reached the proper recipient! During the winter months he regularly took holidays abroad. In his last years he was visited by his doctor every morning and advised whether or not he was fit to get up! As anxiety for his health increased his sojourns in the South of France became lengthier, and it was while staying at Bealieu-sur-Mer that he passed away on 21st April 1909.

The Earl's funeral, held on 4th May at Fletching, attracted mourners from far and wide, special trains being provided from London and Brighton. His body was carried on a gun carriage, the coffin being draped with a Union Jack and decorated with flowers. The Earl was clearly regarded with great affection by many people regardless of their social status and he received a befitting send-off.

As a result of the Earl's death the Earldom became extinct and a glorious era in the history of Sheffield Park came to a close. It is thought that due to his extravagance and considerable generosity he died insolvent. Ownership of the estate passed to Mr. Arthur Gilstrap Soames who immediately began to plant the great collection of trees and shrubs which now give the gardens their special horticultural interest. Distinguished visitors, including Royalty, continued to visit the estate. During the Second World War the mansion and much of the Park was requisitioned by the War Department and later saw use as a repatriation centre for German prisoners. From 1950 onwards the estate was broken-up, the Sheffield Arms Hotel and Mid-Sussex Creamery being among the first interests to be sold-off. This process continued for some years, the gardens eventually coming into the hands of the National Trust in 1955.

77. The 11.30am Lewes to East Grinstead train approaches Ketches bridge, shortly after leaving Sheffield Park, in early March 1958. A variety of locomotive types worked the line during the last few months of its operation by British Railways, but in the author's opinion a single LB&SCR coach hauled by a Class C2X best typifies the line in its twilight days.

P.S. Leaver

78. Nearly twenty years after the previous picture was taken, the scene from the same viewpoint on 29th January 1977 remains much the same, apart from the removal of the telegraph poles. The (then) new Sheffield Park advanced starting signal can just be glimpsed behind the bushes on the right. The 'train' is headed by 'Dukedog' 4-4-0 No. 3217, *Earl of Berkeley*, which had been specially repainted in BR livery and renumbered 9017, in order to simulate a Cambrian lines freight train of the 1950s. The locomotive was out of use, awaiting overhaul, at the time and had been pushed into position by another locomotive which had been discreetly hidden from view. The smoke from the chimney was produced by burning a few oily rags in the smokebox. *John Goss*

79. One of the most rewarding aspects of the current preservation scene is the movement of locomotives between the various private railways. During the winter of 1994/95 the Severn Valley Railway's Ivatt Class 2MT 2-6-0 No. 46443 was 'on tour' in the south of England, and visited a number of lines, including the Bluebell. Sadly, its sojourn at Sheffield Park was all too brief, but at least it had a high profile during the 'Branch Line Weekend' in February and 'Enthusiasts Weekend' the following month. It is seen here on 18th February, during the former event, working the 4.30pm departure from Sheffield Park. Unfortunately, since the previous photograph was taken this area has become somewhat overgrown, and now looks rather neglected. The gradient post, visible in the other pictures, is still *in situ*, but hidden by undergrowth. The field beyond the right-hand fence looks rather bare without the trees, but at least the mature trees on the left survived the 'Great Storm' of 1987 without damage. *John Goss*

80. BR Standard 2-6-4T locomotive No. 80064, which was on loan to the Bluebell for an extended period, 'blows off' as it passes beneath Ketches Bridge with a northbound train on 17th June 1984. Note the abundant foliage which has gained a foothold in crevices in the bridge's brickwork. *J.G. Mallinson*

81. During the 1980s Ketches Bridge was in a steadily worsening state of repair, and in 1987 an engineer's report suggested that urgent repairs costing an estimated £10,000 were necessary. The Railway's management reluctantly decided that such expenditure on an unused bridge could not be justified, and it was agreed that demolition was the only realistic option. This was undertaken by a party of Royal Engineers who blew-up the decaying structure with plastic explosives on 6th October 1987. The resulting explosion, which reduced the bridge to rubble in a few seconds, rocked the normally tranquil surroundings of Sheffield Park. On 28th January 1995 SE&CR C Class 0-6-0 No. 592 is seen passing the site of Ketches Bridge with a train bound for Kingscote. *J.G. Mallinson*

2. Just three weeks before the end of normal services on the line an Ivatt 2-6-2T No. 41317 climbs Freshfield bank with the 4.3pm Lewes to Horsted Keynes train, which is formed of comfortable Bulleid rolling stock. Today, this is a popular spot for photographers who endeavour to obtain that elusive 'master shot' as trains labour up the bank. Apart from the loss of the two mature trees in the field on the right, and telegraph poles, this location has not altered much over the years. The distant wooded horizon is almost unchanged, so if a preserved Ivatt tank engine visits the Bluebell at a future date this photograph could virtually be repeated. *D. Cullum*

Freshfield Bank

3. Hauling a motley collection of coaches, Class P 0-6-0T No. 27 (formerly *Primrose*) assists the graceful Adams 4-4-2T No. 488 up the last few yards of Freshfield bank. They were powering the 3.55pm Sheffield Park to Horsted Keynes train, the attractively named *Wealden Rambler*, on 6th June 1965. The first vehicle in the train is the L&NWR Observation Car, which has since been restored to its former glory. *P.J. Lynch*

84. In early March 1958 the 10.28am East Grinstead to Lewes train rounds the curve at Freshfield and passes beneath Town House bridge as it heads to its next station stop at Sheffield Park. Note the locomotive is displaying an incorrect headcode. Motive power is provided by Class C2X No. 32440 from Brighton shed. *P.S. Leavens*

85. The decision to demolish, in October 1992, the disused Town House bridge dismayed many Bluebell members. The Railway's management cited the critically deteriorating condition of the bridge, and estimated repair cost of at least £10,000, as ample justification for the decision. The money, it was stated, could be used much more effectively on other projects. Critics of the decision argued that the bridge was as much a part of the Railway's heritage as *Birch Grove* or the Observation Saloon and any proposal to dispose of an artefact should at least be made known to the Railway's general membership prior to implementation. Sadly, only the abutments of the bridge now remain, and are seen here in December 1994. *Author*

86. Another completely 'Brighton' train is pictured, on this occasion passing Otye bridge and forming the 10.28am *ex*-East Grinstead on 30th September 1957. The combination of a Class C2X, No. 32437 on this occasion, plus a LB&SCR coach was certainly common during the months of the token service and was highly appropriate to the route. Otye is an accommodation bridge, doubtless built to placate a farmer whose property was severed by construction of the railway.

J.C. Beckett

87. 1980 was the Bluebell's twentieth year of operation, and a number of events were staged to commemorate that anniversary. One of these took place during the first weekend of August when many celebrities and local dignitaries were invited to travel on 'The Pioneer', a special two-coach train which was a re-creation of the Bluebell's first public train which ran 20 years before. Unfortunately, not all the original items of rolling stock were available for use and substitutes had to be used, but even so it successfully rekindled past memories. Here, on 2nd August 1980, *Bluebell*, assisted by *Fenchurch* at the rear, crosses Otye bridge with a Horsted Keynes to Sheffield Park train. It is difficult to believe it is the same location, but the railings on the bridge and gradient post prove conclusively that this is indeed the same spot. Otye bridge has since been infilled.

John Goss

88. On a summer's day in 1970 No. 323, *Bluebell*, coasts across Allen's bridge with a train bound for Sheffield Park. Allen's bridge, situated just south of Holywell, had been in steadily deteriorating condition during the 1980s, and in 1987 the Bluebell Railway's management agreed that repairs costing £5,000 were necessary. At about the same time however, Ketches bridge, near Sheffield Park, was also found to be in need of repairs. It was decided to demolish it, and use the rubble to infill Allen's bridge, which was unused, thus saving considerable expenditure. These operations were carried out during October 1987. Today, apart from a small section of the parapet at the top of the embankment, there is little evidence that a bridge ever existed at this location.

Mike Esau

89. A rare picture of a BR goods train on the Bluebell! Class C2X No. 32539, hauling the 8.32am Lewes to East Grinstead pick-up goods on 30th April 1955, is seen crossing Allen's bridge, the left-hand parapet of which is almost totally obscured by the locomotive's exhaust. The short length of the train will be noted.

J.J. Smith

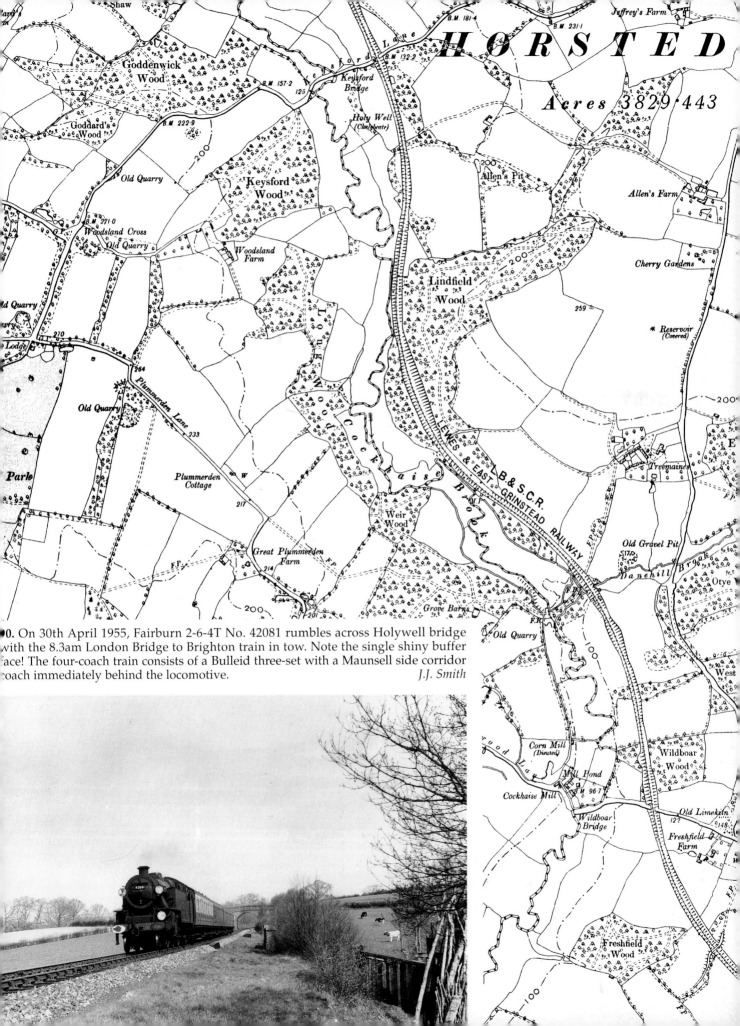

HORSTED

Acres 3829·443

0. On 30th April 1955, Fairburn 2-6-4T No. 42081 rumbles across Holywell bridge with the 8.3am London Bridge to Brighton train in tow. Note the single shiny buffer face! The four-coach train consists of a Bulleid three-set with a Maunsell side corridor coach immediately behind the locomotive.

J.J. Smith

91. A view looking north from the bridge at Holywell in early March 1958, just prior to the cessation of services. *P.S. Leavens*

Holywell

92. When this picture of the current scene was photographed in December 1994 the bridge was undergoing extensive renovation, hence the plastic sheeting and components lying around. The structure itself has been temporarily stripped of its wooden parapet. The general scene has not greatly changed over the years, though the fogman's hut, in front of the signal, has disappeared, together with the lineside telegraph poles. *John Goss*

93. Holywell (Waterworks) Halt was by far the most elaborate of the Bluebell's three original halts, but also the most short-lived. *K. Marx*

Right from the start of the Bluebell enterprise a substantial body of members contended that a halt should be erected at Holywell because it was on the Southdown bus route from Haywards Heath to Horsted Keynes. During the winter of 1961-62 a group of members laboured continuously, despite some particularly bad weather, and the structure was completed during March 1962. It was probably the most elaborate halt the Bluebell ever had, boasting a covered waiting area for passengers and even a small booking office, facilities undreamed of by luckless passengers using Freshfield, the next halt down the line towards Sheffield Park. The halt was opened by the late Lord Beeching, famous pruner of branch lines, on 1st April 1962. Alas, most of the passengers did not come by bus, but by car, which caused congestion on the adjacent road which is little more than a country lane. Consequently, the Bluebell

came under fire from the police and local authorities who wanted the entrance to the halt moved to a safer location. Unfortunately, there was no easy solution to the problem, but nevertheless the halt remained open during the 1962 season under strict control by Bluebell staff.

The problems caused by the building of Holywell Halt were out of all proportion to its usefulness, a grand total of fifty tickets reportedly being issued during the 1962 summer season! During the winter of 1962-63 the Bluebell continued to be under constant pressure from the local council, and became resigned to the fact that it would be unwise to reopen the halt for the 1963 season and advised the authorities accordingly. The halt was dismantled during the 1963-64 close season, and the various timbers and sleepers put to better use elsewhere on the railway.

94. For obvious reasons, photographs of Holywell Halt are uncommon. Class E4 0-6-2T No. 473, later *Birch Grove*, is seen drawing to a halt(!) with a southbound train during the autumn of 1962, shortly after the engine's arrival at the Bluebell. Apart from the loss of the first two digits of its BR number and painting out of the BR logo, the E4 is in 'as delivered' condition. There appear to be at least four prospective passengers on the platform. In view of the halt's very poor passenger usage during its one operational season this would seem to constitute something of a record, or were they merely taking photographs? *J.C. Beckett*

95. On 30th July 1961, Nos. 55, *Stepney*, (front) and 27, *Primrose*, (rear) power the 1.40pm Sheffield Park to Horsted Keynes (Bluebell Halt) train up the 1 in 75 gradient past Holywell. The train is formed of the ancient 'Chesham Set' of coaches bought from London Transport earlier that year. This set, which was the mainstay of the carriage fleet during the Bluebell's early years, was originally built at the turn of the century for the Metropolitan Railway. It was later converted for electric operation which involved adapting the outermost compartments of some vehicles as driving cabs, complete with driver's controls and large end look-out windows. The leading vehicle of the train depicted has been modified in this way. During 1940/41 the set was reconverted for steam working on the Chesham branch, where it remained until electrification in 1960. These vehicles are now amongst the oldest preserved coaches in the country and are currently undergoing extensive restoration.

J.J. Smith

96. Railway photographers have probably complained for generations about one of the most common natural phenomena, namely the sun's nasty habit of disappearing behind a tiny cloud just as a 'master shot' of a passing train is about to be taken. On New Year's Day 1995, however, when the photographer was waiting to take the 2.0pm *ex*-Sheffield Park at Holywell, the sun broke through an otherwise overcast sky just at the right moment, and this striking image resulted. What better start to the New Year could a railway photographer wish for?

John Goss

7. On Saturday 18th/Sunday 19th February, 1995 the Bluebell staged a 'Branch Line Weekend' during which the atmosphere of a branch line in the bygone days of steam was recreated. The event was unfortunately overshadowed, to some degree, by the temporary closure of the section north of Horsted Keynes due to a landslip, which had occurred during a prolonged spell of very wet weather. This resulted in the published timetable being recast at very short notice. On the Saturday the sun shone for most of the day, and an excellent turn-out of visitors (and photographers!) resulted. Here, in glorious afternoon lighting, the 3.10pm Sheffield Park to Horsted Keynes train is seen passing Holywell with C Class No. 592 in charge. The train is formed of a banana van, two SE&CR third-class non-corridor coaches and a LM&SR six-wheel brake van, No. 32975. The latter was making its first appearance in traffic following restoration. *John Goss*

One of the greatest tragedies associated with the Bluebell line occurred near Holywell on the night of 31st July 1943. Earlier that day Gunner Ronald Knapp, aged 22, of the Royal Artillery, of Haywards Heath married Corporal Winifred Standing, aged 21, of the Women's Auxiliary Air Force, of Nobles Farm, Holywell, at St. Giles' Church, Horsted Keynes. Described as a very close and loving couple despite the enforced wartime separation, Gunner Knapp had taken fourteen days leave to marry his sweetheart before going overseas. Following the service at St. Giles' the wedding party returned to Nobles Farm, opposite Holywell Waterworks, for the wedding reception. At 7.50pm the groom's parents had to leave the reception to catch the Southdown bus back to Haywards Heath, and were accompanied to the bus stop at the waterworks by the bride and groom. It was raining heavily at the time and Mr. Standing, the bride's father, lent the group two mackintoshes to protect them from the worst of the downpour. In order to avoid the track to the farm, which was in very muddy condition, the party walked along the railway line for about 100 yards. At about 8.20pm Mr. & Mrs. Knapp senior boarded the Southdown bus to Haywards Heath. Little did they know it then, but that was the last time they were to see their son and daughter-in-law alive.

A few minutes later, at 8.32pm, the 7.34pm Brighton to East Grinstead train pulled out of Sheffield Park station. The precise movements of the newly-married couple when they left the bus stop are not known, but when the train passed the roadbridge at Holywell at about 8.42pm the guard, Mr. Percy Whittington, of Hove, noticed something lying in the 'four-foot' of the track. Upon arrival at Horsted Keynes he informed the driver, and together they examined the train and found a mackintosh on the front buffer beam. Mr. Albert Miles, sub ganger of the local permanent way department, was called to search the track and discovered two bodies about three-quarters of a mile south of Horsted Keynes station. He also found a second mackintosh about half a mile away from the station.

At the inquest the train driver, Mr. William Whiting, of Brighton, stated that on the night of the incident his train ran into a severe rainstorm shortly after leaving Sheffield Park, making visibility very poor. He said that when the train passed Holywell he was not especially looking out, particularly in view of the driving rain. Asked by the coroner how he thought one mackintosh had come to be on the engine the ganger was of the opinion that they were probably wearing one mackintosh over both their heads. Other witnesses stated that at the point where the accident happened there was no public access to the railway and all the fences were in a good state of repair. A verdict of accidental death was recorded, the coroner, Dr. E.F. Hoare, noting that the deceased were trespassing on the line as he suspected many others had done previously at this location. He concluded that they were probably walking with their backs to the oncoming train with one mackintosh over both their heads which prevented them hearing its approach. He exonerated all the railway staff involved from any blame whatsoever.

Ten days after the wedding the couple were laid to rest in St. Giles' churchyard and their tidy graves remain as a sad reminder of the tragedy which struck on that wet Saturday night.

98. The view from the bridge just north of Holywell offers a reasonably good panorama of the surrounding countryside and also Bluebell trains as they round the curve and commence the stiff climb towards Horsted Keynes. Here a northbound working is seen in the early 1960s, with an engine at each end of the train.

T.J. Edgington

99. Steam power personified! Class 9F No. 92240 creates a powerful image as it attacks the climb with a six-coach train in tow on Boxing Day, 1994. Apart from the loss of the telegraph poles, this location has seen few changes, and remains a popular spot for photographers.

John Goss

00. During the 1950s Bulleid Pacifics occasionally visited the line in charge of ramblers' excursions, which usually originated in London. n 22nd March 1953, 'Battle of Britain' Class No. 34071, *601 Squadron*, passes beneath the lofty overbridge in Nobles Farm cutting, just outh of Horsted Keynes, with a train for Sheffield Park. Note the white buffers, and generally clean condition of the locomotive. *S.C. Nash*

01. Three Arch Bridge is no longer the most oteworthy landmark on the Bluebell ollowing the reopening of Sharpthorne nnel, but even so remains a prominent piece f infrastructure. Apart from the S&T cable nction box and water container, this view oks much the same as it did forty years ago. he deteriorating condition of the bridge's rickwork will be noted, and remedial action nnot be long delayed. The train is headed y L&SWR M7 Class 0-4-4T No. 30053, and is photograph was taken on 5th March 1994, uring one of its sorties on line work.

J.G. Mallinson

102. The evening light glints beautifully on the side of the train, as the Adams tank locomotive, assisted by *Stepney*, approaches Horsted Keynes (Bluebell Halt) with a train from Sheffield Park in October 1961.

D.B. Clark

Bluebell Halt

103. The Adams locomotive waits at Bluebell Halt prior to returning to Sheffield Park. The Maunsell BCK vehicle, No. 6575, appears to be in use as a waiting room/booking office and close inspection of the picture reveals that it is protected by a red flag.

D.B. Clark

104. During the early spring of 1967 Universal Pictures took over part of the line for the filming of 'I'll Never Forget What's-'is-Name' which starred Orson Welles and Oliver Reed. Produced by Michael Winner, the film centred on the activities of an advertising agency and part of the film taken on the Bluebell showed the agency staff making an advertising film. For this purpose Bluebell Halt was converted into a ghost station and the North London Tank locomotive plus two Chesham coaches were painted white to resemble a ghost train. Here the film-makers are seen taking a break between sessions, with their ghost station and train prominent in the background.

M.J. Mason

105. *Bluebell* stands at Bluebell Halt on 5th February 1962 *en route* to Sheffield Park with two newly-delivered coaches, a 'Birdcage' brake and a LC&DR six-wheel vehicle. Note the cupboard housing the telephone apparatus, visible at the far end of the platform, which provided communication with the signalman at Sheffield Park. The wooden fence, which separated Bluebell from BR property, and footpath from the roadway are just discernible. *M.J. Mason*

106. The ghost train in action certainly made a weird sight, perhaps not the sort of train you would want to see coming into a shadowy, dimly-lit station on a dark night.

M.J. Mason

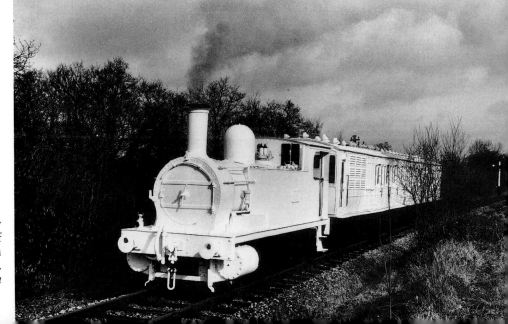

107. The resumption of passenger services in August 1956 once again provided an opportunity for railtours over the hitherto moribund route, a point which was not lost on the enterprising Locomotive Club of Great Britain. It arranged a tour for 24th February 1957 which is seen here leaving Horsted Keynes with C2X Class No. 32437 in charge. This locomotive had just replaced LB&SCR Atlantic No. 32424, *Beachy Head*, which succumbed with big-end trouble. The tour, which started from Marylebone, had originally been scheduled for haulage by *Beachy Head* from Clapham Junction to Portsmouth via Brixton, the Mid-Kent line, Sanderstead, East Grinstead, Lewes and Brighton. A visit to Brighton Works and a 'Terrier'-hauled trip to Hayling Island and back also featured on the itinerary, before participants were treated to a fast run to Waterloo along the Portsmouth Direct route. The fare for this splendid day out was twenty-seven shillings.
N.W. Sprinks

108. Hauling a rake of immaculate Bulleid coaches, with a Maunsell brake formed at the rear, the Bluebell Railway's ancient LB&SCR A1X Class 0-6-0Ts, Nos. 72, *Fenchurch* and 55, *Stepney*, leave Horsted Keynes with a train to Sheffield Park on 12th September 1982. Nicknamed 'Terriers', on account of their ability to accelerate rapidly, these are among the oldest nominally operational preserved locomotives in Great Britain. Except for removal of the loading gauge, and water tank atop the pumphouse, this view has not greatly changed.
John Goss

109. In superb autumn lighting conditions *Stepney* pilots the Adams 'Radial' tank locomotive into Horsted Keynes station with the 2.46pm *ex*-Sheffield Park on 29th October 1961. This was the first day of through running into Horsted Keynes. *Bluebell* and *Primrose* are out of sight at the rear of the train. Note the large number of wagons in the yard. It is possible, however, that they were stored and not in revenue-earning service.

G. Daniels

110. Few features from the old days now remain at the south end of Horsted Keynes station. Remnants of the old track layout have survived and the course of the Ardingly branch is still visible, but little else. The carriage shed, a small part of which can be seen on the left of the picture, was completed in 1971 on the site of the former goods yard. This has probably had more visual impact on Horsted Keynes than any other development. The water crane, in the middle of the picture, and viewing area in the foreground, are more recent additions to the scene. The vehicles on the right provide essential sleeping accommodation and mess facilities for volunteers. The train depicted is a 'Santa Special' hauled by Class 9F No. 92240, and the photograph was taken on 4th December 1994.

John Goss

111. A LB&SCR E4 class 'Large Radial' tank locomotive, believed to be No. 2491, runs alongside the main London to Brighton line at Copyhold Junction. The train is a three-coach rake of SE&CR origin. The exact date of this photograph has not been recorded, but it appears to have been taken in about 1933. The main-line tracks are electrified and a colour light signal is clearly visible in the distance, on the Ardingly branch.

Lens of Sutton

Ardingly Branch

112. *Birch Grove* and the Adams 'Radial' approach Copyhold Junction during their run from Sheffield Park to Haywards Heath to collect the 'Scottish Belle' railtour on 15th September 1963. The train had been worked down from Victoria by the Caledonian Railway 'Single' No. 123 in tandem with L&SWR T9 Class No. 120. Both visiting engines worked down to Brighton shed for turning purposes prior to going on display at Horsted Keynes during the afternoon. They later returned the excursionists to the Capital. *W.A.C. Smith*

13. A Victoria to Brighton express train (identified by the headcode, which denotes [a] fast service) approaches Copyhold Junction on 31st January 1995. The single-track [b]ranch to the Ardingly stone terminal is on the right. Apart from the obvious track [a]lterations, the scene has not changed greatly over the years. There is, however, one [s]ubtle change that is not apparent from the photograph, and this concerns the main [li]ne tracks which are now reversible lines, signalled for running in both directions. [T]o facilitate bi-directional running, crossovers are provided at both Copyhold and [B]alcombe Tunnel Junctions, and at other points on the double-track sections of the [B]righton line. This alternative method of working, which is usually used in an [e]mergency, or because of trackwork, was introduced when the Brighton line was [r]esignalled in 1985. The train is formed of an unusual eight-car unit (classified 8-DIG [o]r Class 422/0) which is generally confined to the express services between London [a]nd Brighton.

John Goss

114. 'Ardingly for Ardingly College' states t[h]
station nameboard on the up platform, as if [to]
stress the importance to the railway of th[e]
traffic generated by the nearby public scho[ol.]
This picture was taken on 3rd March 19[5?]
before the arrival of electric trains, or indee[d]
judging by the platform oil lamps, electric lig[ht.]
The Ardingly branch was built primarily [to]
provide improved connections between Sou[th]
Coast towns and settlements along th[e]
secondary route to London via East Grinstea[d.]
It was also hoped that a rail connection wou[ld]
eventually lead to the expansion of Ardingl[y]
which would become a lucrative source [of]
traffic for the railway. Unfortunately, the bran[ch]
never fulfilled the expectations of its promoter[s]
and it came as no surprise when it was close[d]
in 1963.   *Bluebell Archiv[e]*

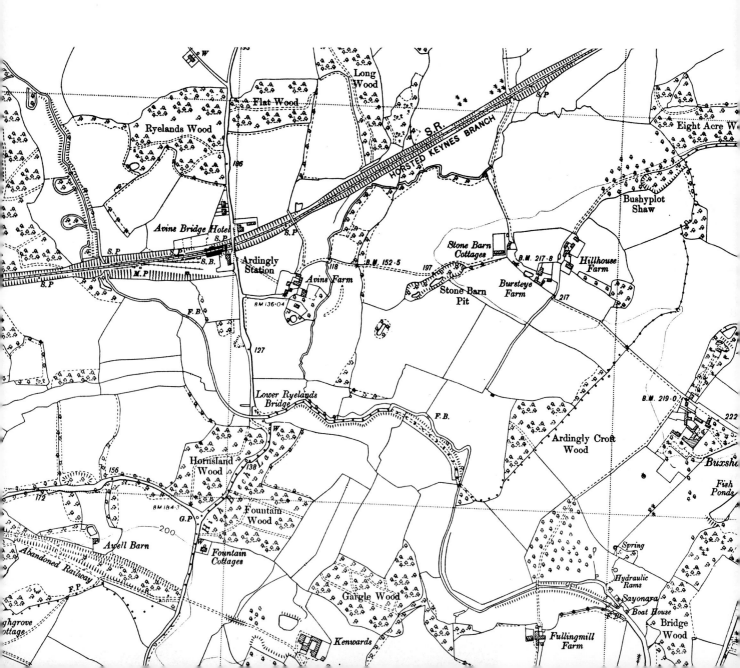

15. On 31st March 1963 the Bluebell organised a railtour from Victoria to Sheffield Park which was powered as far as Haywards Heath by BR Standard tank locomotive No. 80084 piloting *Birch Grove*. There the Adams 4-4-2T No. 488 was attached to the rear of the train and *Birch Grove* remained on the front while No. 80084 proceeded to Brighton shed for servicing. The train then set off for Horsted Keynes with the Adams 'Radial' leading and *Birch Grove* on the rear. Here the train is seen passing Ardingly *en route* for Horsted Keynes. Note the stone terminal on the left and some elderly stone wagons in the yard.

D.B. Clark

16. Much of the former station area and goods yard at Ardingly are now the site of a stone supply depot owned by the Amey Roadstone Corporation. Unfortunately, owing to building developments at the site, it was not possible for the photographer to take a picture from exactly the same spot as the previous illustration. Note the section of the down platform (in the left foreground) from where the previous picture was taken. The photographer, therefore, had to be content with this general view of the yard. It is interesting to see a large quantity of railway sleepers in the picture, even if they are not being used for their original purpose!

J.G. Mallinson

117. The main station building at Ardingly, photographed in the 1950s. *D. Cullum*

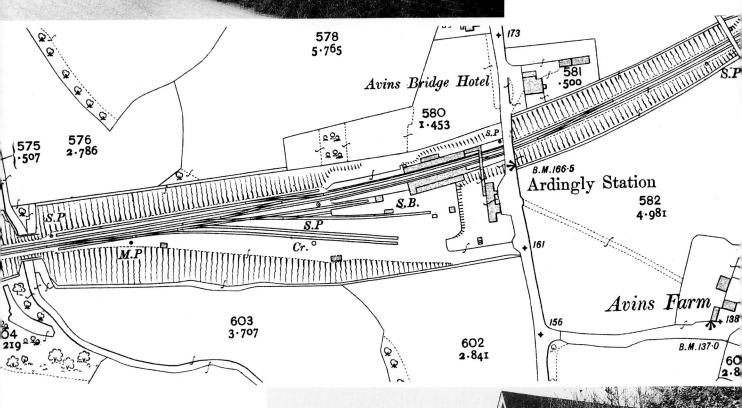

118. In 1994 the main station building at Ardingly was still extant, and it continues to be in a good state of repair. When viewed from the same angle as the previous picture there is, however, little to be seen, due to the presence of a large group of trees. The adjacent brick wall is still in place. *J.G. Mallinson*

119. The sparsity of regular steam workings along the Ardingly branch following electrification has resulted in a dearth of photographs. Consequently, all the action pictures featured in this section are of special workings. The 'Victory Belle' ran on Trafalgar Day, 21st October 1962, and like most Bluebell railtours started from Victoria. The 350 participants were powered along the Brighton line as far as Haywards Heath by the preserved L&SWR T9 Class 4-4-0 No. 120. There *Stepney*, piloting the Adams 'Radial' tank locomotive No. 488, took over for the run to Horsted Keynes, and the pair are pictured here passing Ardingly on the outward run. Note the first three vehicles of the train each represent a different era of carriage construction. The first is a nondescript brake vehicle built in the late 1920s for use on Continental boat trains, while the second and third vehicles are of BR Standard and Bulleid design respectively. The tail lamp is still in position on the first coach (which would have been on the rear coming down from London). Perhaps the guard had forgotten to remove it while the train was changing engines at Haywards Heath. *D.B. Clark*

120. Will *Stepney* or the Adams 'Radial' locomotive ever pass this way again? The trackbed is clear, but the sides of the cutting are now hidden by a mass of trees, shrubs and brambles which have clearly run riot over the years, and denied the photographer access to the position from which the previous photograph was taken. At least the bridge still survives, although now almost completely concealed from view. *J.G. Mallinson*

121. The winter of 1962/63 was one of the most severe in living memory, and large patches of snow still linger on the ground as SR Q1 Class 0-6-0 No. 33018 hauls a train of condemned stock towards Ardingly station on 24th February 1963. The train is travelling along the former up line, which became a bi-directional single line when the adjacent down track was taken out of use as a running line in 1959. The latter was used for the storage of new electric multiple-unit stock destined for the Kent Coast lines. Later a wide selection of condemned SR steam stock of various types replaced the electric units, being dumped on the branch prior to scrapping.

D.B. Clark

122. The east portal of the 215 yards-long Lywood Tunnel. The 'train' visible at the other end of the bore is actually a line of withdrawn locomotive-hauled coaches. *D. Cullum*

Lywood Tunnel

123. Despite more than thirty years of disuse the trackbed is remarkably clear, and tyre tracks suggest that it is in regular use, presumably by the landowner. The portal is now partly covered by ivy, moss and even one or two small shrubs, which have found a niche for themselves. The brickwork is still in a reasonably sound condition, though it would benefit from repointing! Clearly, if the Bluebell or BR ever wish to reopen the line, laying track here would be a relatively straightforward operation, but judging by the pools of water something would need to be done about the drainage. This scene was recorded in January 1995. *John Goss*

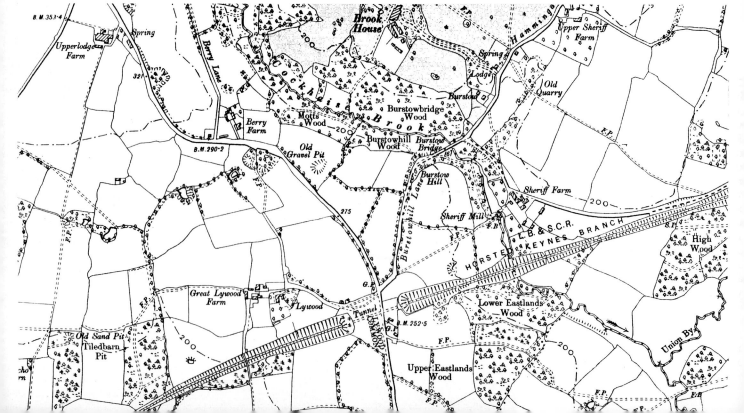

125. A passenger's eye view of the approach to Horsted Keynes a few days before closure of the Lewes to East Grinstead route. *R. Hobbs*

4. *Opposite*: A demolition train would not normally be considered a [pr]omising subject for a photograph, nor perhaps a suitable one, but in this [pi]cture the photographer has got everything 'just right' and a picture of [ex]ceptional quality has resulted. This scene was recorded during the [su]mmer of 1964 when track removal on the Ardingly branch was in full [sw]ing. The photograph depicts the Bluebell Railway's splendid LB&SCR [E] Class locomotive No. 473, *Birch Grove*, heading towards West Hoathly [wi]th three wagons of track panels in tow. The eastern portal of Lywood [tu]nnel can be seen in the background. *R. Hobbs*

Horsted Keynes

[12]6. *Birch Grove* at Horsted Keynes with a [Sh]effield Park train on 16th August 1964. [A]t this time the station was still in BR [ow]nership although no longer served by [B]R trains following closure of the Ardingly [br]anch in October 1963. Nature was clearly [do]ing its best to take over, judging by the [pr]ofusion of weeds sprouting between the [tr]acks. Note the up Ardingly branch track [o]n the extreme left) had recently seen use, [in]dicated by the shiny rail surface. At this [ti]me track-lifting was in progress on the [A]rdingly branch and materials were being [co]nveyed by rail to West Hoathly goods [ya]rd from where they were taken away [by] road, or rail via East Grinstead. The [N]orth London Railway tank locomotive [N]o. 2650 (latterly BR No. 58850) was being [em]ployed on track-lifting duties at this [ti]me and can be seen apparently being [co]upled to *Stepney* at the rear of the train. *E. Wilmshurst*

127. The layout seen here is that which was brought into use in June 1914 following the transfer of t
junction from the north to the south end of Horsted Keynes station. The bracket signal controlling
trains off the Ardingly branch and which is just discernible in the middle of the picture, indicates t
the principal route for trains off the branch was to Platform 2. Unfortunately the exact date of t
photograph is unknown. *D. Bowley, S. Baker collect*

Examples abound of grand junction stations constructed in the middle of nowhere by over-optimistic railway companies for traffic which never materialised. Horsted Keynes is a classic example, its inevitable decline beginning only thirty years after its opening in 1882!

Originally, there were four platforms in regular use, numbers 1 and 2 being the up and down Ardingly lines respectively on the western-most island platform, which had waiting rooms and a canopy. Trains to and from Sheffield Park were dealt with at the other platforms, number 3 being for northbound services while the double-sided track was used by southbound trains. The junction between the two routes was located at the north end of the station and controlled by the north signal box, which was situated on the down side, while the south box – which is still extant – controlled the tracks at the southern end of the station.

This layout and relatively complex method of operation lasted for

some years, but in 1913 the LB&SCR decided that four platforms a
two signalboxes could not be justified, bearing in mind the amount
traffic on offer, and drew up plans to reduce the layout and passen
facilities. These hinged around moving the junction from the north
the south end of the station, a proposal which would enable the no
signal box to be reduced in status to a shunting frame. Platform
formerly the up Ardingly line, was closed to passenger traffic a
became a siding. The remaining platforms were consequen
renumbered, Platform 2 becoming number 1 and so on. This platfo
remained in regular use for up trains from Ardingly and also the
which terminated at Horsted Keynes. They had to proceed north of
station to use a trailing crossover which enabled them to reach Platfo
3 whence they returned to Ardingly and beyond.

continued oppo

128. In 1935 the layout underwent furth
alterations in order to accommoda
terminating electric trains, the electrifi
tracks being readily identifiable in t
view recorded on 8th March 1958. No
the alteration to the track serving t
dock siding, which was presumab
another change dating from the mi
1930s. *D. Cull*

129. Following withdrawal of BR passenger services in 1963 and the subsequent purchase of the entire site by the Bluebell Railway, it was inevitable that the old junction layout would disappear. The change took place on a piecemeal basis over many years, the latest development being in late 1994 when the connection from Platform 2 to the former goods yard (now the carriage shed) was removed. Access to the yard is now only available via the single slip on the left of the picture. The course of the Ardingly branch is now a storage area for rolling stock which is accessed from a siding behind the signal box. The signal box has survived all the changes unscathed, but was fortunate to escape severe damage when struck by lightning during a storm in July, 1980. The strike knocked off the chimney stack which hit an adjacent coach before landing. *Author*

ntinued from previous page Through trains on the Ardingly route used e eastern-most platforms, a radical departure from previous practice. 1ese changes are believed to have been introduced on 26th June 1914. r the passengers, the track alterations probably went almost 1noticed, the most dramatic change for them being the total removal all buildings from the downgraded western-most platform, which ade that side of the station look rather uninviting. It is thought that is measure was carried out in order to give the signalman in the ormer) south box an unimpeded view of movements. In addition to e trackwork alterations previously described, access to the up sidings the north end of the station was also altered. One side effect of the anges was the uprooting and repositioning of some telegraph poles!

Twenty years elapsed before any more substantial modifications were ade to the track layout at Horsted Keynes. The year 1933 saw auguration of the Brighton line electrification and two years later the es to Seaford, Eastbourne and Ore were similarly treated. In addition the 'East Coast' lines, it was also decided to electrify the short section om Haywards Heath to Horsted Keynes. It is unclear whether the uthern Railway authorities expected an upsurge in passenger traffic on the branch to result and more likely that the decision to electrify the branch was for operational reasons. An hourly service to Seaford was provided initially. The electric trains from Horsted Keynes connected at Haywards Heath with a down Brighton service and also a Victoria – Ore train, which they followed from Haywards Heath to Southerham Junction, east of Lewes, before branching off to Seaford. Unfortunately, the track layout which existed at that time did not permit bi-directional running so it was essential that at least one platform road was provided with this facility in order to avoid the time-consuming movements previously described and also additional installation costs. It was decided that Platform 1 would be electrified and a new crossover provided immediately south of the signal box. At the same time the connection from the up Ardingly line into Platform 2 was removed. A down starting signal was also installed at the south end of Platform 1. Down trains could still reach the Ardingly branch by means of the crossover from Platform 3. This revised layout survived from 1935 until the closure of the Ardingly branch in 1963 and indeed much of the disused trackwork remained *in situ* for many years following the Bluebell's takeover.

130. A fascinating view of Horsted Keyn taken from the top of the pumphou water tank. Unfortunately the precise da of the picture is not known, but it w presumably taken during the Secor World War, judging by the blank statio nameboards, and ships' propellers in t foreground. A present day view of th scene from the same position would l interesting, but is unobtainable owing the removal of the water tank from the t of the pumphouse.

D. Bowley, S.R. Baker Collectic

131. A 4-LAV electric unit, No. 29 waits to leave Horsted Keynes 7th May 1955 with a 2.3pm footb special to Hove, hence the unusu headcode, not normally used trains from Horsted Keynes, whi is the same as the old Victoria Littlehampton (via Hove) code. N the scaffolding around the stati house: the latter presumably w being repainted. Sidings n occupy the area in the foregrou and berthed rolling stock norma obscures most of the platforms a station. *D. Cullu*

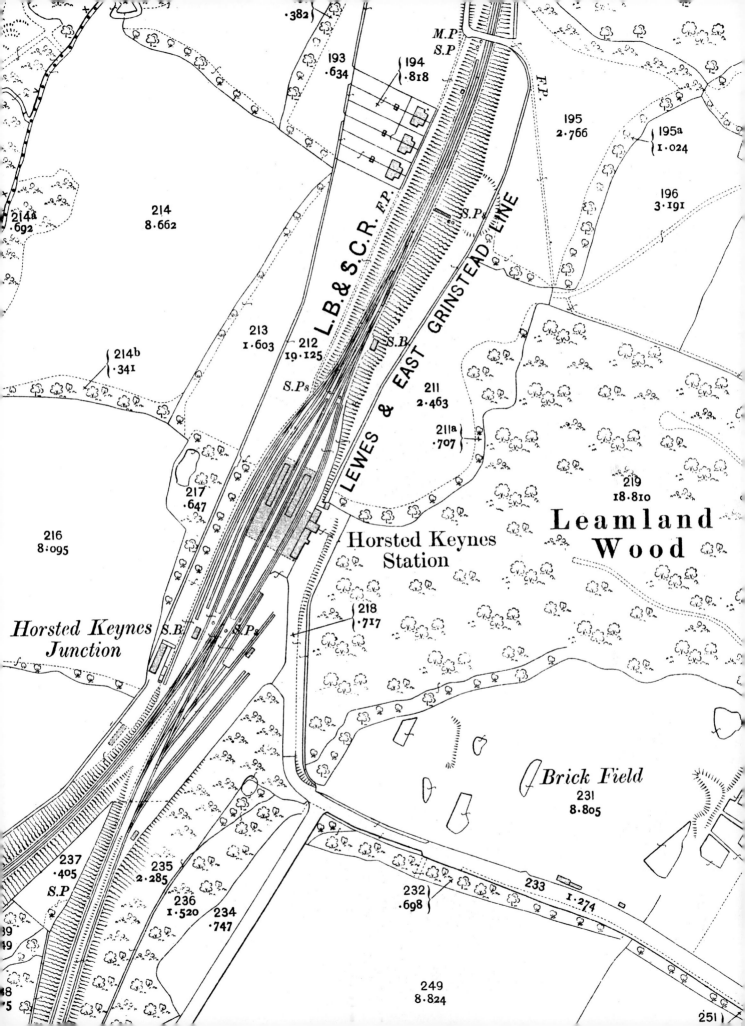

.382

193
.634

194
.818

M.P
S.P

F.P

195
2.766

195a
1.024

196
3.191

214a
.692

214
8.662

S.Ps

L.B.&.S.C.R. F.P.

S.B

LEWES & EAST GRINSTEAD LINE

211
2.463

211a
.707

214b
.341

213
1.603

212
19.125

S.Ps

219
18.810

Leamland
Wood

217
.647

216
8.095

Horsted Keynes
Station

Horsted Keynes
Junction

S.B.

S.Ps

218
.717

Brick Field
231
8.805

237
.405

S.P

235
2.285

236
1.520

234
.747

232
.698

233
1.274

249
8.824

251

132. The 11.20am West Hoathly to Lewes freight train, with tender-first class C2X No.32540 in charge, reposes at Horsted Keynes on 23rd October 1953. It is thought that by this time the daily goods train from Lewes usually travelled as far as Kingscote, but on this occasion it is quite possible there was no traffic from there and it turned around at West Hoathly.

N.W. Sprinks

133. If railway preservation is all about keeping alive the atmosphere of steam railway travel and conserving the environment and artefacts, judging by this view of Horsted Keynes station on 18th February 1994, the Bluebell Railway is succeeding brilliantly. The train, hauled by M7 Class 0-4-4T No. 30053 (which had been temporarily disguised as No. 30124) was a 'Sentimental Journeys' charter special. A few minor alterations have been carried out at the station, but basically it remains much the same as it was forty years ago, and rightly so. What a pity the graceful M7 Class locomotive is not a permanent resident at Sheffield Park!

J.G. Mallinson

134. The frontage of Horsted Keynes station is seen from the approach road on 8th March 1958. Note the recently pollarded trees beyond the fence. *D. Cullum*

135. This view of Horsted Keynes station has changed little over the years, apart from the addition of some enamel signs on the fence, and hanging baskets on the front of the station building, which hardly mar its appearance. The most noticeable alteration occurred in 1976 when a roadway was built to link the approach road with the 'Top Field' which had been purchased by the Bluebell some years previously. This involved removing a number of mature trees and constructing a culvert for a diverted stream. The field is now used as a car park, also as the venue for a variety of events each year, and must rank as one of the most sound investments the Bluebell has ever made. *J.G. Mallinson*

136. A ten-coach ramblers' special enters Horsted Keynes on 8th September 1957, hauled by 'Battle of Britain' Class Pacific No. 34068 *Kenley*. Note the two L&SWR 'Ironclad' coaches immediately behind the engine: these vehicles were quite rare on the Central Section

N.W. Sprink

137. Ivatt Class 2MT 2-6-0 No. 46443, which was on loan from the Severn Valley Railway, was photographed in the course of running round its train (which is out of the picture) at Horsted Keynes on 19th February 1995, during the Bluebell's 'Branch Line Weekend'. The growth of the trees adjacent to the cottages is the most striking difference between the two scenes. The railway cottages seem to be in a much better state of repair than they were in 1957.

John Gos

138. This splendid photograph of L&SWR Class T9 4-4-0 No. 30718 leaving Horsted Keynes has been published before, but it is one of the author's all-time personal favourite Bluebell photographs; this (at least in his view!) is ample justification for using it again! Everything seems to be right, soft evening lighting, a commendably clean locomotive, plus the superb background of the station and wooded hazy horizons beyond, all combine to produce a real gem of a picture. Careful examination will reveal a connecting electric unit just setting off past the signal box *en-route* to Seaford. The date was 25th May 1955, and the train was the 5.18pm from Brighton to Victoria.

J.J. Smith

139. Nearly forty years on from the date of the previous picture, the idyllic setting of Horsted Keynes station is unchanged, and long may it remain so. The station's immediate environs have altered considerably however, the most remarkable changes being the laying of additional sidings to accommodate the Bluebell's burgeoning rolling stock collection, and erection of the carriage shed. Despite these necessary intrusions Horsted Keynes remains one of the most ornate and picturesque stations on any preserved railway. This photograph depicts BR Standard Class 9F No. 92240 leaving with the 3.30pm from Sheffield Park to Kingscote on 30th December 1994.

John Goss

140. One of the most memorable occasions in the history of Horsted Keynes station since the Bluebell started operating occurred on 15th September 1963, when the beautiful Caledonian Railway Single locomotive No. 123 piloted a railtour from Victoria. Built by Neilson & Co. of Glasgow in 1886, No. 123 ran in ordinary service in Scotland until 1935 when it was laid aside in St. Rollox Works. After the war No. 123 made occasional appearances at various events as a static locomotive, but in 1958 the Scottish Region restored it to full working order for use on special trains. The famous locomotive was brought down from Scotland specially for the Bluebell excursion and drew a crowd of about 2,000 admirers to Horsted Keynes. The special's train engine was L&SWR T9 Class No. 120 which, it must be admitted, provided most of the power, but No. 123 certainly stole the show!

W.A.C. Smith

41. A view looking south towards the overbridge at Horsted House farm on 31st March 1990, giving some idea of the scale of the clearance work required to clear the trackbed of the line, which nature had steadily reclaimed during twenty-five years of disuse. Note that half of the arch has been bricked-up in connection with the installation of a rifle range. At this time, phase one of the Northern extension had already been completed as far as the other side of the bridge, a 'push-pull' style shuttle service from Horsted Keynes being the method of operation. *J.G. Mallinson*

42. 'Merchant Navy' Class Pacific No. 35027, *Port Line*, hauling the 2.10pm Sheffield Park to Kingscote train, pounds uphill as it passes beneath Horsted House farm bridge on 29th August 1994. The bridges on the section of line north of Horsted Keynes are of a different pattern to others on the line, and appear to be more sturdily constructed. This example is built of a combination of stone and brick, which is particularly attractive. *Port Line* came to the Bluebell on loan in the summer of 1988 and has been based at Sheffield Park ever since.

J.G. Mallinson

143. The Bluebell Railway's North London Railway tank locomotive, No. 2650, propels a short train along the up line south of Sharpthorne Tunnel on 29th July 1964. Note the carpet of weeds which had become established during the line's long period of disuse. The wagon nearest the locomotive appears to be loaded with firewood, presumably for steam-raising purposes!   *S.C. Nash*

The Northern Extension

The tale of the Bluebell Railway's Northern Extension is long and complex so it is intended to present only a condensed version of events in this album. The full story would, perhaps, justify a book in its own right. The first major event occurred in 1974 when the owners of the West Hoathly station site applied for planning permission to develop the site. Before that time many members had felt that because of the Bluebell's short five miles long section of track the railway might not retain its public appeal in the long term and envious eyes were often cast towards more recently established lines which offered a longer journey. Furthermore, in the early 1970s oil supplies had been under threat and the Bluebell, where the vast majority of visitors arrive by car, was seen to be in a vulnerable position. So, it was therefore decided that unless development at West Hoathly could be prevented, any future hope of a main line connection at East Grinstead would be lost for ever. Clearly the only option would be for the Bluebell to intervene and purchase the land themselves. Protracted negotiations with the site owners took place and in late 1975 were successfully concluded. On 30th November the West Hoathly site became the property of the Bluebell!

But four months later the plans of the newly-formed Bluebell Extension Railway Ltd. suffered a major setback when the Mid-Sussex District Council rejected an application to extend the line to West Hoathly. A further application to extend the railway to East Grinstead was similarly rebuffed, and it became clear that a full public inquiry into the Railway's plans would be needed in view of the vociferous opposition of local farmers and landowners. The inquiry took place in June 1983 at Haywards Heath, and a searching examination of the Railway's plans took place. The next milestone occurred during the summer of 1984 when Kingscote station unexpectedly came on to the market. Despite the fact that the result of the inquiry was still awaited the courageous decision was taken to purchase the property for £102,000. Thus the railway now owned both of the former station sites, but none of the land in between!

In April 1985 the Secretaries of State for the Environment and Transport announced the crucial decision upon which the Bluebell's hopes depended. The answer was 'yes', the railway was granted planning permission to extend to East Grinstead and a Light Railway Order. Everyone involved in the project no doubt breathed tremendous sighs of relief. Having successfully negotiated the first hurdle the Extension Company now faced an even more challenging task, that of raising the money to finance the project. On 14th March 1986, the Bluebell launched a public share issue. The success or failure of that flotation was the litmus test of public support for the Bluebell scheme, but the railway also overcame this hurdle, the magnificent total of more than £450,000 being raised. While these events took place in the full glare of publicity, behind the scenes delicate negotiations with landowners continued and more and more land was being acquired, and it was clear that the start of physical work on the extension would soon be a possibility.

In early 1988 volunteers set to work clearing the trees and undergrowth just north of Leamland bridge, Horsted Keynes, and the project was on its way! In March 1988 a ceremony marking the formal start of reconstruction took place at the same spot and the railway was honoured by the presence of the (then) Secretary of State for Transport, the Rt. Hon. Paul Channon MP, who ceremoniously laid the first section of track using the steam crane. The work schedule for the first phase of the extension up to Horsted House bridge, illustrates the complexity of the undertaking:

i)   Clear all trees and growth on the trackbed and culverts unless required for screening. Aim: *Completion by August 1988.*

ii) Grading of formation, removal of tree stumps and repairs to embankment, new drainage and work up to sub-ballast. Aim: *Completion by early 1989.*

iii) Lay ballast, sleepers and rail, with a view to passenger traffic (a small engine and one or two coaches propelled) by early summer. Aim: *Operation by May 1989.*

The above details refer to the first three quarters of a mile of reclaimed trackbed north of Horsted Keynes, which had no major engineering problems. It is interesting to note that the land immediately north of Horsted Keynes had only been acquired by the Bluebell four months previously! The whole rebuilding operation from Horsted Keynes to East Grinstead was divided from the outset into seven separate phases and it was on this initial section where volunteers 'cut their teeth'. One of the first problems to be solved was that of road access for materials and equipment. A new track for this purpose was installed just north of Leamland bridge using 100 tonnes of brick rubble. This was one of the notable achievements of the early days. Most of the work during the first year of the project involved clearance of trees which had sprung up during the thirty years that the line had been dormant. Other tasks included removal of spoil from both ends of the trackbed, balancing the flood relief pond by Leamland bridge, regrading Horsted House Farm cutting and the demolition of the remaining sheep pens in the same area. The start of work on the extension attracted new working members and the early arrival of a JCB excavator greatly assisted progress.

Another major area of activity centred on the fencelines, most of which were clogged with undergrowth, which had to be removed before any work could be done on the fences themselves. The Railway is obliged by statute to ensure all its property is suitably fenced so this was a vital part of the rebuilding operation. It was quickly discovered that most of the posts required replacement and all the wire had to be renewed – a Herculean task in itself.

November 1988 saw the start of two other tasks, namely the removal of trees from the embankment sides in order to stabilise it, and the start of work on the drainage system. The latter task involved the installation of a completely new system, largely due to defects in the old installation and years of neglect in the years since closure. After years of

continued opposite

negotiations, legal argument and fund-raising the first section of the extension, up to Horsted House Farm, was starting to look more like a railway again. By April 1989 the formation was ready to receive the new track – the great moment had arrived!

Before any ballast could be laid it was necessary to set out the line of the track using, in this case, about 100 pegs. A line of route just east of the centre of the trackbed is deemed to be the only practical position for the new track. It is worth noting that due to civil engineering considerations the original 1 in 75 gradient had been substantially altered by BR, much of it now rising steeply at 1 in 62. It was decided to save expense and move all the track components into position using road vehicles before laying ballast. For the record 1,200 sleepers, 2,400 chairs and some 2,000 tonnes of limestone ballast were used. The ballast, ordered from Amey Roadstone at Ardingly, came from a quarry near Frome, Somerset, and arrived on a special train. The operation of laying the track was programmed to start on the 3rd, and end on 29th April, 1989. This exacting schedule was maintained without too many hiccoughs and at about 5pm on the 29th, Class Q locomotive No. 541 formed the first train to traverse the rebuilt stretch of line for twenty-five years, cheered by a large group of modern-day navvies. On the first section at least, dreams had become reality after fifteen years of waiting!

But the heartening news that the first phase of the extension had been finished on time was tempered by the fact that introduction of the shuttle service, originally envisaged to start in May 1989, would not take place as planned. An upsurge in the on-train catering business necessitated the installation of a separate siding, at Sheffield Park, completion of which was delayed by signalling problems. In addition, a D.O.T. requirement that operation of the proposed extension shuttle should be independent from the rest of the railway resulted in additional track and signalling alterations at Horsted Keynes which could not be completed in time to allow introduction of the planned shuttle service in 1989. Consequently this was unavoidably delayed until Easter 1990.

The formal introduction of the shuttle took place on 14th April 1990 following a D.O.T. inspection the previous day. Due to the lack of a run-round facility at the terminus the train, which operated from Horsted Keynes independently of the main service, had to be propelled up the gradient in the northbound direction. To facilitate this, the brake-end of coach No. 6575 was fitted with an observation window and communication through the train with the driver. The prospect of a run north of Horsted Keynes along a route which had been a dense 'jungle' until two years previously proved an irresistible attraction to the public who made nearly 8,000 journeys in just twelve days! Apart from the start of the shuttle, another major development at about this time was the agreement on terms with the owners of the trackbed through Courtland Wood. This section of route, from Horsted House Farm bridge to Sharpthorne tunnel, was the last between Horsted Keynes and Kingscote to be acquired by the railway. A further landmark on the operational front occurred on 30th June when 'Schools' class 4-4-0 No. 928, Stowe, assisted in the rear by Bluebell, headed the first non-stop train through Horsted Keynes for 29 years! One unexpected and unwelcome development during the late summer of 1990 was the discovery of a fire on the east side of the railway about half way along the completed section of the extension. It was judged that it had been started by the burning of scrub and undergrowth and this in turn had ignited combustible material, including ash, which had been tipped there in steam days. In March 1991 work started on digging out the fire which, fortunately, did not extend under the track. After five days of hard work the fire had been extinguished and the site excavated. The affected area was then filled with a mixture of grit, the remains of the fire and the original inert embankment, with each layer being compacted back into the excavation.

Apart from successfully resolving the fire slip problem, the Bluebell's other major task during the early part of 1991 was to raise more money to finance building of the line right through to Kingscote, phases two, three and four of the extension. To achieve this objective a second share issue was launched on 14th February, St. Valentine's Day, using a London firm of public relations consultants. Coverage in national and local press, television and radio ensured a fanfare of publicity which was essential if the Railway's plans to reach Kingscote were to be realised. Bearing in mind that the launch was made during one of the most severe economic recessions ever experienced, the Bluebell did well to reach a figure of almost £170,000 after two months. This amount had swelled to almost £300,000 by the end of 1991.

Construction of the second phase of the operation – from Horsted House Farm bridge to Coombe Farm bridge – was seen initially as a slightly easier section to work on. The trackbed was much clearer than

anticipated and the drainage in reasonable condition. The cost of rebuilding this section was estimated to be £230,000, the vast majority of this amount being the cost of permanent way materials. An idea of the scale of operation can be gauged from the fact that almost 4,000 tons of ballast had to be purchased for phase two and this arrived in 164 lorry loads! The ballast arrived during August 1991, being delivered to a newly-established base at West Hoathly. Originally, it had been intended to lay the ballast for the whole of phase two in one operation, but this plan was thwarted by a serious embankment slip at Vaux End, north of Horsted House Farm bridge. Consequently, ballast was laid on only the northern section of phase two while the problem of the slip was addressed. Various ideas were proposed before a party of civil engineers, who were paying a visit to the site, suggested the use of geotextiles. These are layers of plastic mesh which, if installed correctly, artificially increase the natural strength of the soil, which in this case was the notoriously unstable Wealden clay. Over 4,000 tons of material was excavated during a four day period of non-stop activity in early September 1991. Altogether sixteen layers of mesh were used as the clay was recompacted back into the embankment. The whole operation went like clockwork; even the weather was on its best behaviour, nearly two weeks of unbroken sunshine being experienced. Despite this considerable additional workload, construction continued apace during the autumn. Another major headache encountered was a geological fault south of Sharpthorne tunnel. This required stabilising in order to create a firm base for the ballast and track and 800 tonnes of rock were used for this purpose.

The first few months of 1992 were, if anything, even more hectic than the last months of the previous year as track-laying continued as fast as conditions allowed. The next major milestone occurred at 4.45pm on 5th March when B4 class 0-4-0T, Normandy, emerged from the northern portal of Sharpthorne tunnel, the first train through since 1964! To give the whole task a really professional finish a Plasser-Theurer tamper-liner machine was hired from the Midland Railway Centre and a ballast regulator from the Kent and East Sussex Railway, which took all the hard work out of shovelling the ballast. Before regular operations commenced the loop at West Hoathly had to be laid including the installation of two turnouts. This work was completed by 26th March. For the record an amazing total of over 300 trains were run from Horsted Keynes to the site of work, conveying track materials. In all 3,500 tons of ballast were carried, 1,800 sleepers and 300 rails, the latter being acquired from a colliery in the Midlands. On 13th April 'Merchant Navy' class Pacific No. 35027, Port Line, hauled a special test train up to New Coombe bridge to test clearances preparatory to the official inspection by Major Olver, HM Inspecting Officer of Railways, the following day. He gave the new section of railway his approval and an impromptu special was run from Sheffield Park at 2.00pm on 14th April. This was the first public train through Sharpthorne tunnel for more than thirty years. Three days later scheduled public services commenced and the Bluebell had achieved another major goal on its way to East Grinstead. The 'official' reopening took place on 16th May when Sir Alastair Morton, Chairman of Eurotunnel, was the principal guest.

The dust had hardly settled on the second stage of the project when work commenced on phase three – the installation of New Coombe bridge. The structure had been obtained some years previously from North Wales, but before it could be put in place abutments had to be constructed. These rested on piles drilled from the top of each embankment. The bridge itself consists of a three-span structure, each span being nine metres long. The two supporting intermediate piers are prefabricated steel trestles. It was originally proposed to erect the bridge during December 1992, but heavy rain during the preceding weeks sabotaged the plan. Piling work was proposed for February 1993, but the firm engaged unfortunately went into voluntary liquidation a fortnight before it was due to start. Another firm was found and the work arranged for late March. This time the piling actually started, but came to an abrupt halt on the first day when a spring was discovered! Despite these reverses, work continued and the structure was completed, albeit somewhat behind schedule, on 10th May. The final cost amounted to £43,000, a fraction of the outlay that would have been required had the bridge been designed and built commercially.

Following the successful conclusion of the first three stages of the extension, completion of the next phase, as far as Kingscote station, may have seemed a formality. It was clear, however, that without considerable cost savings on the projected expenditure and more funds becoming available, the objective of reaching Kingscote by March 1994 was beginning to look unattainable. The total estimate for phase four was

continued overleaf

144. In March 1990, when this photograph was taken, this permanent way hut near Courtland Wood, south of Sharpthorne tunnel, probably resembled many more similar structures on abandoned railway lines up and down the country. A footpath indicates the course of the line, but everywhere else nature has run rampant, completely taking over the trackbed...

J.G. Mallinson

continued from previous page £260,000 of which the lion's share was the cost of ballast (£85,000), sleepers (£60,000), and rail fittings (£21,500). A steady flow of funds continued, however, as a result of the generosity of shareholders and preparatory work continued on the section of line north to Kingscote. Vast quantities of ballast from Hoo Junction, near Gravesend, were stockpiled at Kingscote in readiness for tracklaying. Laying of the ballast commenced in early January 1994, working down from Kingscote, and track laying started shortly afterwards. Atrocious weather delayed the operation, but despite this most of the work had been completed by mid-February, when only the final stage into the station remained outstanding. This could not be completed due to planning difficulties which were not resolved until 30th March. The trackwork in the station was finished during the Easter holiday, and on 19th April Major Poyntz, of the Railway Inspectorate, passed the new section of railway for public use.

Despite initial doubts that funding would be available, Kingscote was reopened in good time for the 1994 season as originally planned – another magnificent achievement by the extension team. The first train ran on St. George's Day, with the formal opening on 21st May. The principal guests were Major General Sir Philip Ward, Vice Lieutenant of the County of West Sussex, who described the occasion as a 'great historical moment', and Councillor Wilf Knighton, Chairman of Mid-Sussex District Council.

In this comparatively short *resume* of the extension story to date, no attempt has been made to cover all the activities which have come together to bring the success the scheme has so far achieved. The extension has brought a massive increase in the workload of the Bluebell's dedicated signalling and telecommunications department, for example, while the detailed negotiations with landowners and local authorities is a vital area of the exercise which is unseen and often unrecognised. What, then, are the prospects of reaching East Grinstead before the turn of the century? It could be said that the Bluebell has a mountain to climb, the mountain in this case being Imberhorne tip, north of Kingscote. So far the extension project has cost £1.35m. and at least £1m. will have to be spent on removing the tip, provided, of course, a suitable 'hole' is found. In addition, there will be substantial outlay on track and a new station at East Grinstead. This is a formidable challenge and clearly the Bluebell will need all the experience and expertise gathered during twenty years if it is to succeed, coupled with an abundant supply of funds. Let us wish them well.

145. ...but, only two years later a complete and startling transformation had taken place. As a result of the herculean effort made by the extension team, trains were running again by April 1992, a tremendous achievement by any yardstick. It is probably difficult for the layman to fully comprehend the amount of work necessary to restore a stretch of railway, but perhaps the incredible contrast between these views will give some idea of the endeavour required to achieve the remarkable rebirth of this piece of line.

J.G. Mallinson

Sharpthorne Tunnel

146. On the penultimate day of services, 15th March 1958, BR Standard Class 4MT 2-6-4T No. 80011 emerges from Sharpthorne tunnel with the 2.28pm East Grinstead to Lewes train. *J.C. Beckett*

147. The following day the same photographer was again on hand to record the 2.28pm from East Grinstead at West Hoathly and on this occasion selected a highly unusual vantage point taking his shot from just inside the northern entrance to the tunnel. The sunny conditions and polished condition of the locomotive, not to mention the imaginative location, have combined to produce an exceptional picture spoilt only by the engine's strange homemade headboard. This view gives an excellent indication of the change of gradient which occurs at this point, the nominal 1 in 75 climb from Horsted Keynes finishes just as West Hoathly station is reached, enabling firemen to take a well-earned rest.

J.C. Becket

148. Between 1964 and 1992 Sharpthorne tunnel remained abandoned and both entrances became blocked with undergrowth which formed an almost impassable barrier. At least one intrepid photographer penetrated this jungle, however, and took this picture looking out of the northern portal, on 12th June 1983. L&SWR B4 Class 0-4-0T, *Normandy*, made history when it hauled the first train for twenty-eight years through the tunnel, on 5th March 1992.

J.G. Mallinson

49. For obvious reasons Sharpthorne tunnel is now strictly out of bounds to photographers and special permission had to be obtained for this photograph to be taken. Here, visiting L&SWR M7 class 0-4-4T No. 30053 is seen as it is about to plunge into the cavernous depths of the tunnel with a Kingscote to Sheffield Park train in October 1994. There is no doubt that being hauled through a damp, eerie and echoing tunnel by a steam locomotive, with billowing smoke and steam reflecting the orange glow from the fire, is a unique experience that is not easily forgotten. *J.G. Mallinson*

Victorian railway contractors frequently began new undertakings with tunnelling work, so it is not surprising that when the navvies set to work building the Lewes and East Grinstead Railway, construction of Sharpthorne (West Hoathly) tunnel was a top priority. Digging a tunnel was not only a very protracted, laborious and labour-intensive operation, but also an invaluable source of vast quantities of spoil which could be used elsewhere on the formation to build embankments, obviating the need to purchase similar material at additional expense. In late 1878 the local press reported that 600 men were at work on the construction, and no accidents had occurred up to that time. This creditable fact was attributed to the care of Mr. Kirby, the superintendent, who was said to be a 'most experienced tunnel maker'. It was reported that five shafts had been sunk for the purpose of expediting the work, and an engine for hoisting and lowering materials was in place above each one. The preliminary driftway was almost complete from one end to the other. The report mentioned that the tunnel passed through a very hard dark blue clay of the Wealden series which required blasting when underground. When brought to the surface the material soon became soft after a little exposure to the atmosphere. This property attracted the attention of local geologists who apparently had not previously seen such material in the neighbourhood. The driftway referred to in the article was in fact broken through on 14th January 1879.

The scene atop Sharpthorne ridge during work on the bore must have been absorbing, because in addition to the five steam hoists raising and lowering earth and equipment there were numerous horses transporting materials to and from each shaft. The tunnel mouths would also have been a veritable hive of activity with skips loaded high with earth emerging from the blackness while others stacked full of bricks waited outside to be pushed into the tunnel. Underground, and largely unseen, navvies would be digging away with picks and shovels at the tunnel work-face, quickly ferrying spoil in baskets to the nearest available skip. Following behind the navvies were carpenters who quickly shored-up the newly-excavated section before it had a chance to cave in! The carpenters would then be followed by the bricklayers who needed all their skill and expertise to lay the lining walls and then install the curved tunnel roof.

Despite the close supervision of the superintendent referred to earlier, some accidents did occur, causing loss of life on at least one occasion. The fatal accident involved Henry Mighal, a native of Sharpthorne, who was employed as a bricklayer's labourer when the incident happened on 1st December 1879. He was working on a section of the arch work in No. 3 shaft in the centre of the tunnel when the wooden centres, which

support the arches, gave way while in the course of being turned. The unfortunate victim was crushed by the wooden beams and died before he could be moved out of the tunnel. Some weeks earlier, on 11th October 1879, another navvy was fortunate to escape with his life when a newly-laid section of brickwork collapsed onto him, dislocating his shoulder and breaking a leg.

Sharpthorne tunnel is best remembered though, not for triumphs and tragedies during construction, but for the size of the icicles which had to be removed during cold winters. Two local landowners, Mr. F.A. Du Croz and General Arbuthnot, could be said to have been largely responsible for this because they objected to the original tunnel alignment on the rather spurious grounds that it would have interfered with their hunting and game-shooting! Their protests caused the route of the tunnel to be altered slightly, but the new alignment proved an unmitigated disaster, as it took the bore through a labyrinth of underground springs which cascaded their water through the lining of the walls and roof. There was even a well above the tunnel! The West Hoathly end was the worst, and during some winters icicles 'as big as human bodies' sometimes stretched down from the roof to rail level, particularly if a freezing north-east wind was blowing into the portal. It became part of the daily routine for platelayers to enter the tunnel and break off the icicles with sledgehammers or any suitable tool available. Engine crews, particularly on early morning trains, were always aware of the danger from large icicles, and stood together in the middle of the footplate while they passed through the bore. Passengers have always been warned 'not to lean out of the window' and mercifully no instances have been recorded of them being injured as they travelled through the tunnel.

During February 1954 an intrepid reporter from the *East Grinstead Courier* was permitted to walk through the tunnel to experience what he described as 'the truly arctic conditions' which prevailed during that month. He saw massive eight feet-long icicles hanging from the roof; it was he said, 'a veritable fairyland... the curved walls were one mass of ice formations, making all manner of fantastic shapes'. On one occasion during that bitter February a gang of fifteen men struggled all night long to clear the tunnel of an estimated 100 tons of ice, but as soon as they cleared one icicle another would form nearby as accumulated seeping water quickly froze. In the harsh winter of 1947, one of the worst in living memory, the local gangers cleared so much ice it filled a train of 49 ballast wagons! But perhaps the most remarkable fact of all about Sharpthorne tunnel is that following a twenty-eight years period of disuse it was reopened in 1992, and is the longest tunnel on a British preserved railway.

150. An unidentified BR Standard tank locomotive plunges into the depths of Sharpthorne tunnel with a southbound train during a snowstorm on 8th March 1958. *E. Wilmshurst*

151. West Hoathly panorama! Viewed from a lofty position almost above the tunnel mouth a Fairburn Class 4MT 2-6-4T locomotive No. 42104, makes a brisk departure from the station on the favourable grade. The train is the 4.20pm London Bridge to Brighton formed of two 3-coach sets of 'Birdcage' and Bulleid stock, and the scene was recorded on 27th May 1955, the penultimate day of 'normal' services before a footplatemen's strike took effect. The station approach road is just visible on the left of the picture while the middle background is dominated by the station and brickworks. Beyond lies some glorious Wealden countryside, but unfortunately the dull weather conditions do nothing to enhance its undoubted natural beauty. *D. Cullum*

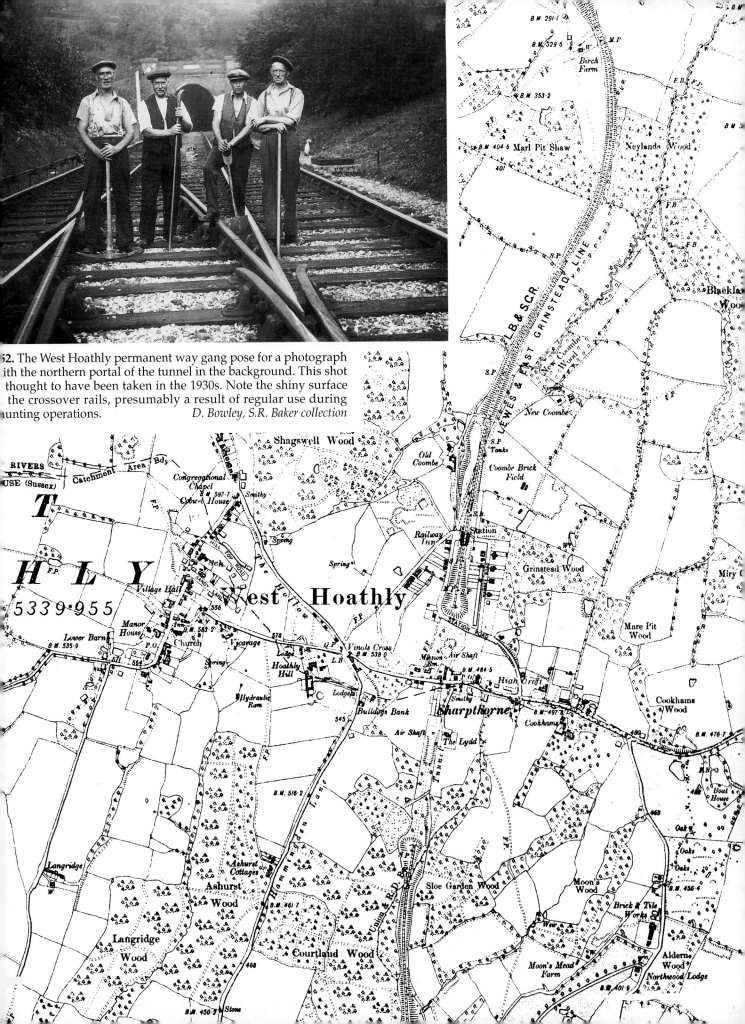

52. The West Hoathly permanent way gang pose for a photograph with the northern portal of the tunnel in the background. This shot is thought to have been taken in the 1930s. Note the shiny surface of the crossover rails, presumably a result of regular use during shunting operations.

D. Bowley, S.R. Baker collection

153. The weather-beaten and rather spindly footbridge at West Hoathly frames BR Standard Class 4MT tank locomotive No. 80032 as it heads through southwards 'wrong line' with a long train of condemned wagons destined for the breaker's yard at Newhaven. The precise date of this picture is unknown, but it is likely to have been taken in January 1960. Note the rows of pollarded trees standing gaunt against the sky. *The late Derek Cross*

West Hoathly

154. The public footpath which crosses the site of West Hoathly station is virtually the only feature of interest in this picture, taken on 4th December 1994. The crumbling remains of the station's platforms at least offer tangible evidence that a station once existed at this spot. Note the drain cover in the foreground which appears to be the original: surely not? *John Goss*

155. The shadows are lengthening at West Hoathly on the beautiful evening of 31st August 1954. *J.H. Aston*

156. The frontage of West Hoathly station on 27th May 1955. Note the ugly modification to the front chimney which spoils the appearance of a splendid structure. The building in the foreground is a public house, which no doubt frequently provided a refuge for weary travellers in days gone by. *D. Cullum*

157. BR Standard Class 4MT tank locomotive No. 80145 pulls into West Hoathly station with a northbound train on 15th March 195̸
Four 'genuine' passengers are waiting on the platform to board the train, which has been strengthened to six coaches to accommoda̸
people making their final journey over the line. Note the smoke belching from the tunnel mouth.   *R. Hobb̸*

During the period of the line's construction West Hoathly was the main centre of activity for many of the navvies employed on the contract. They were billeted in wooden huts sited in a field high up on the ridge, near the road connecting the villages of Sharpthorne and West Hoathly. Hence the apparently odd location of the railway cottages by the road above the tunnel rather than adjacent to the station, or inn, just opposite. Blacksmiths, carpenters, bricklayers and a host of other tradesmen were housed in their simple but distinctive dwellings, while the foremen enjoyed the comparative luxury of two specially-built bungalows, one of which was still standing – albeit in dilapidated condition – well into the 1960s.

One of the most interesting landmarks at West Hoathly is the brickworks located just north of the former station on the east side of the tracks. It is one of the few industrial premises located on the former Lewes to East Grinstead line and is still in production today. It opened in about 1880, when railway building work was still in full swing, and was initially shown on maps at that time as Coombe Brick Field. Later in the 1880s a Mr. Alan Stenning was apparently the proprietor, but by 1899 Mr. W. Hudson had taken over. From 1913 until 1976 the firm was known as Hudsons Ltd then became Ibstock Brick Hudsons. The brickyard was for many years a valued customer of the railway, not only despatching new bricks daily but also wagons of ash and other non-combustible material. The firm enjoyed the luxury of their own siding, long enough to accommodate twenty wagons, which was worked by the signal box off the down line. Unfortunately, in 1954 the firm decided to switch their traffic to road transport and the siding fell into disuse.

It is not clear whether bricks manufactured at the Coombe Brick Field were used in the construction of the railway, because the railway navvies had their own brickyard. This was located on the west side of the line and was thought to have come into operation before the other yard. It was

here that the distinctive red-coloured bricks, which are so apparent on th̸ line's viaducts, bridges, station buildings and tunnel portals, were bake̸

Passenger traffic at West Hoathly was never more than moderat̸ although the platforms would occasionally be busy when a special trai̸ was provided to Lingfield races or a ramblers' special came down fro̸ London. There was, however, a considerable amount of goods traffic, i̸ addition to the consignments from the brickworks already mentione̸ There were two coalyards, which were separately owned, and a lot o̸ traffic of farm produce, especially dairy products. The latter wa̸ lucrative traffic for the railway and a special milk train left at 9 ever̸ morning conveying about forty-five churns from West Hoathly, i̸ addition to consignments from other stations. Freight traffic started it̸ downward spiral in the 1930s, but the war years saw a short-lived reviv̸ During the war Canadian troops were stationed at Courtlands estate whi̸ the attractive Gravetye woods became an ammunition dump whic̸ sometimes necessitated trains running at night – quite a novelty on th̸ stretch of route.

When it became clear that BR saw no future for the line one of the loc̸ coal merchants, Mr. Jack Leppard, was among those who fiercely oppose̸ the closure plans, speaking out fearlessly at the Public Inquiry at Lewe̸ He contested that the replacement bus services proposed were wholl̸ inadequate and in any case buses were unable to convey prams. H̸ considered that better connections with other services and the provisio̸ of more excursions during the summer months could sway the balance i̸ the line's favour. These arguments cut no ice with the railway authoritie̸ however, whose minds already appeared to be made up. Followin̸ closure, the goods sidings were lifted during October 1960, but th̸ through lines survived, with the footbridge and down platform building̸ until 1964. The station house was the final building to be demolished, i̸ September 1967.

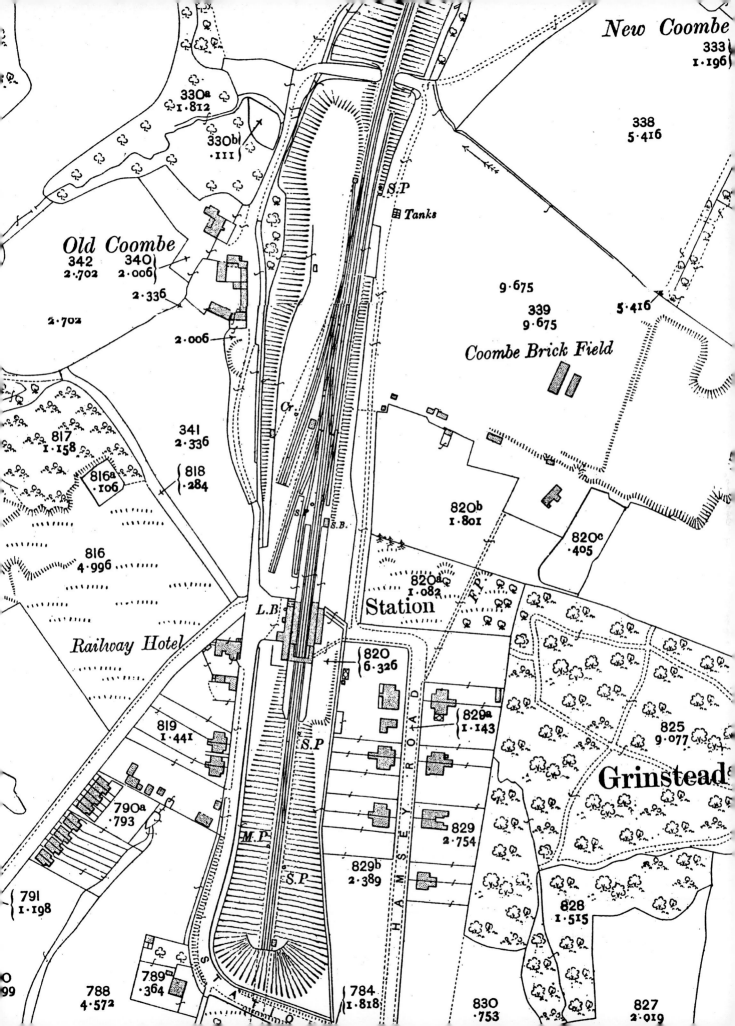

New Coombe
333
1·196

330a
1·812

330b
·111

338
5·416

S.P

Tanks

Old Coombe
342   340
2·702   2·006

2·336

9·675

2·702

2·006

339
9·675

5·416

Coombe Brick Field

Cr.

817
1·158

816a
·106

341
2·336

818
·284

820b
1·801

820c
·405

816
4·996

S.B.

F.P.

820a
1·082

Station

L.B.

Railway Hotel

820
6·326

829a
1·143

825
9·077

819
1·441

S.P

829
2·754

Grinstead

790a
·793

M.P.

791
1·198

S.P

829b
2·389

828
1·515

789
·364

STATION

788
4·572

784
1·818

830
·753

827
2·019

99

158. In the early days of the demolition work the contractors used a small Ruston and Hornsby diesel locomotive to move trainloads of materials, but this soon failed and the Bluebell was requested to provide a replacement steam locomotive. The defective diesel is seen standing on the down line while the substitute North London tank locomotive is just visible behind a short train of track panels on the up line. The wooden shelter on the down platform had already fallen victim to the scrapmen, while the footbridge was in the throes of destruction. Note the shed on the down platform, which was presumably the scrapmen's 'headquarters office', also another, smaller, shed in the wagon behind the diesel locomotive. The latter shed was used as mobile messing accommodation. Scenes like this were common up and down the country at this time due to the Government's policy of closing unremunerative branch lines in an effort to make the railways pay their way. This scene was photographed in October 1964.   *J.J. Smith*

159. The North London tank locomotive simmers gently at West Hoathly prior to its next assignment. Note the pile of coal! A crew for the locomotive was provided by the Bluebell Railway, the engine normally leaving Sheffield Park at 7.0am and returning coupled to the rear locomotive of the 5.25pm from Horsted Keynes. When track lifting commenced north of Horsted Keynes the locomotive became isolated and the enginemen travelled to and from West Hoathly by road. The marooned North London tank later returned from East Grinstead on a low loader.   *J.J. Smith*

60. *Birch Grove* was in use on track lifting duties when this picture was taken at West Hoathly during the summer of 1964.

Bluebell Archives

During the second half of 1964 and early part of 1965, West Hoathly station yard was used as a base by the contractors lifting the line from Ardingly to East Grinstead, exclusive of Horsted Keynes. During this period the yard was a hive of activity, with trains of lifted track panels, powered by locomotives borrowed from the Bluebell, arriving daily. The panels would then be off-loaded and dismantled into their component parts in a similar fashion to the operation at Newick and Chailey five years previously. The rails, sleepers and other fittings were later removed to East Grinstead goods yard for onward movement by rail, or taken away from West Hoathly by road. Many of the components were purchased by the National Coal Board for further use at collieries in the West Midlands.

61. The North London tank stands on the up line at West Hoathly on 23rd January 1965, apparently out of steam, while the crane is at work unloading track panels from the flat wagons. The locomotive has been covered with a tarpaulin to protect it from the worst of the winter weather. The wagons in the distance were presumably used to convey materials to East Grinstead.

E. Wilmshurst

162. Ivatt Class 2MT 2-6-2T locomotive No. 41306 coasts into West Hoathly passing the signal box and rather weather-beaten station nameboard. An asbestos-clad building, part of the brickworks complex, forms the background. This picture was taken on 28t[March 1955.

P. Ha[

163. On 27th March 1994, SE&CR P Class 0-6-0 No. 323, *Bluebell*, hauls the Observation Car an[G.N.R. Directors' Saloon away from the site c West Hoathly station. *Bluebell* had powered 'trial run' special train to Kingscote earlier tha afternoon, but the loop there had yet to b completed, so *Bluebell* was obliged to propel it train back to West Hoathly where it ran-roun[The loop at West Hoathly was removed shortl after this photograph was taken. *J.G. Mallinso[*

164. In a picture full of interest U1 Class 'Mogul' No. 31900 is seen leaving West Hoathly with the 3.28pm Haywards Heath to London Bridge train on 7th May 1955. The train is composed of seven vehicles, with a SE&CR 'Birdcage' set formed immediately behind the locomotive, and a Bulleid three-car set following. The last vehicle is barely identifiable, but appears to be of Maunsell outline. The public house is on the right, opposite the main station building, while two coal wagons and an enormous heap of coal indicate that the goods yard was still in business, even if only just! The former brickworks siding is apparently in use for storing condemned wooden-bodied wagons, while the works itself lies beyond the perimeter fence, largely concealed from view. The scene is completed by the wooded slopes of Sharpthorne ridge.
C. Hogg

165. On New Year's Day 1995, the Bluebell's impressive Class 9F 2-10-0 No. 92240 steams past the empty wasteland formerly occupied by West Hoathly station and sidings. Only the tunnel portal, and mounds of earth on the site of the former platforms and goods yard loading dock, survived destruction by the demolition men. Note the housing development which has occurred in recent years.
John Goss

166. The 9.50am Victoria to Ardingly ramblers' excursion, hauled by 'Battle of Britain' class Pacific No. 34068, *Kenley*, approaches West Hoathly on a sunny 27th September 1959. The first coach was reserved for Bluebell members who were attending a Rally Day at Sheffield Park: this was one of the first events organised by the embryonic Bluebell Railway Preservation Society. One of the first ever ramblers' excursions ran from Victoria to West Hoathly in May 1932 and similar specials operated, usually twice a year, until the outbreak of war in 1939. Workings resumed in April, 1950 when Class N 2-6-0 No. 31816 was provided to work a train of ten coaches. The 'Mogul' lost time and larger locomotives were rostered for subsequent trains which usually ran to Sheffield Park, from where the empty stock continued to Lewes. Following the closure of the Lewes to East Grinstead line the ramblers resorted to electric trains which ran to Horsted Keynes via Haywards Heath, but reopening of the line in 1956 provided a golden opportunity to run via East Grinstead, using steam traction once again. The first of these trains ran in September 1957, also hauled by *Kenley*, but this and subsequent trains served Horsted Keynes and Ardingly, not Sheffield Park. The working seen here is believed to have been the final public service train along the route before its closure to all traffic.   *S.C. Nash*

167. In the author's opinion this section of the line represents a rather depressing part of a journey on the Bluebell. The emptiness of the former station and goods yard sites serves as a brutal reminder of the efficiency of the demolition crew who erased the railway from the landscape at West Hoathly. At least the sound of steam has returned, but somehow the Class 9F, running tender-first while hauling a Santa Special in December 1994, does not quite capture the flavour of the old days. Perhaps, one day, it may be possible to reconstruct the station and restore the various goods facilities. A pipe dream perhaps, but on the Bluebell such dreams have sometimes been realised. Here's hoping!   *John Goss*

68. Class C2X 0-6-0 No. 32442 whisks its single coach train along on the last lap of its journey from West Hoathly to East Grinstead in February 1958. The various dwellings on the top of Sharpthorne Ridge are visible on the horizon. Note the locomotive is displaying a lamp in place of one of the headcode discs.

P.S. Leavens

169. Mill Place is the appealing setting for this portrait of LM&SR-designed 2-6-4T No. 42103 heading south with an afternoon train from Oxted to Brighton on 27th May 1955. There is an attractive bridge (from which the picture was taken) and cutting at this point. This is a particularly beautiful stretch of line which offers outstanding views towards Weir Wood reservoir and the distinctive Wealden scenery beyond. The gradient here is 1 in 122 against southbound trains, one of the few stretches where the firemen of northbound trains can take it relatively easy.

D. Cullum

Mill Place

170. Following closure to regular passenger traffic in March 1958, the section of line from East Grinstead to Horsted Keynes was retained on a 'care and maintenance' basis and saw occasional use by enthusiasts' specials and ramblers' excursions. One of the latter trains is seen here in September 1959 with Bulleid 'Light Pacific' No. 34068, *Kenley*, in charge. The up line of this section of track was used for the storage of withdrawn freight vehicles prior to breaking-up at Newhaven or Polegate, and a line of these stretches as far as the eye can see. Note the growth of lineside vegetation during the period since the previous picture was taken.

J.J. Smith

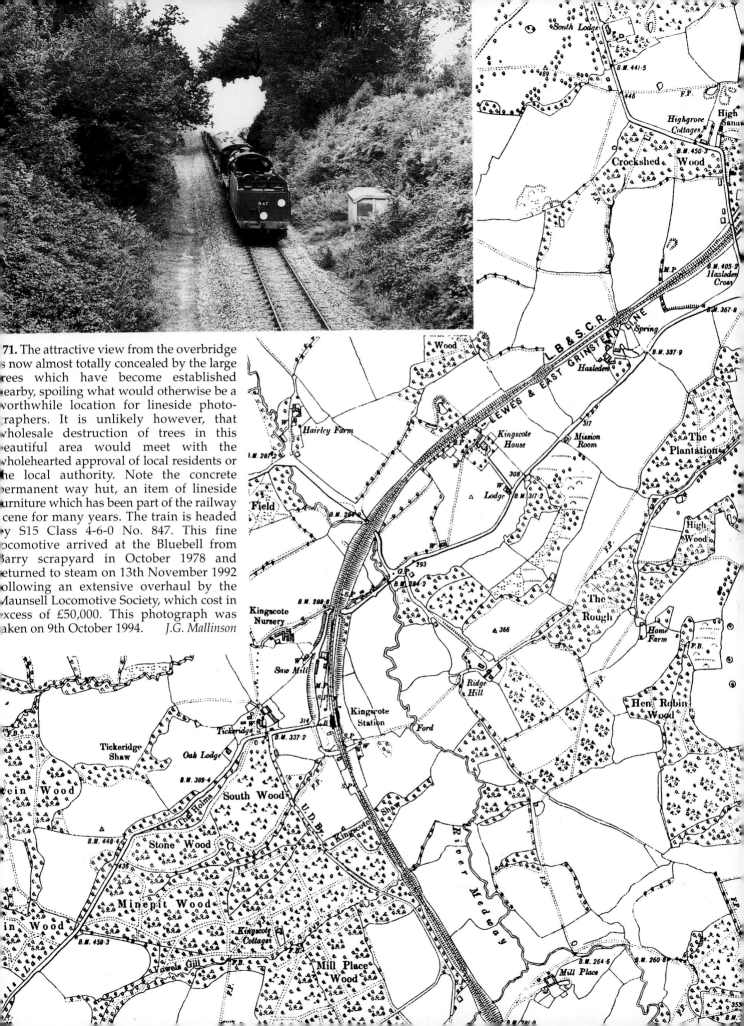

71. The attractive view from the overbridge is now almost totally concealed by the large trees which have become established nearby, spoiling what would otherwise be a worthwhile location for lineside photographers. It is unlikely however, that wholesale destruction of trees in this beautiful area would meet with the wholehearted approval of local residents or the local authority. Note the concrete permanent way hut, an item of lineside furniture which has been part of the railway scene for many years. The train is headed by S15 Class 4-6-0 No. 847. This fine locomotive arrived at the Bluebell from Barry scrapyard in October 1978 and returned to steam on 13th November 1992 following an extensive overhaul by the Maunsell Locomotive Society, which cost in excess of £50,000. This photograph was taken on 9th October 1994. *J.G. Mallinson*

Kingscote

172. Class N 'Mogul' No. 31853 coasts downhill towards Kingscote with the 3.28pm Haywards Heath to London Bridge train on 27th May 1955.
D. Cullum

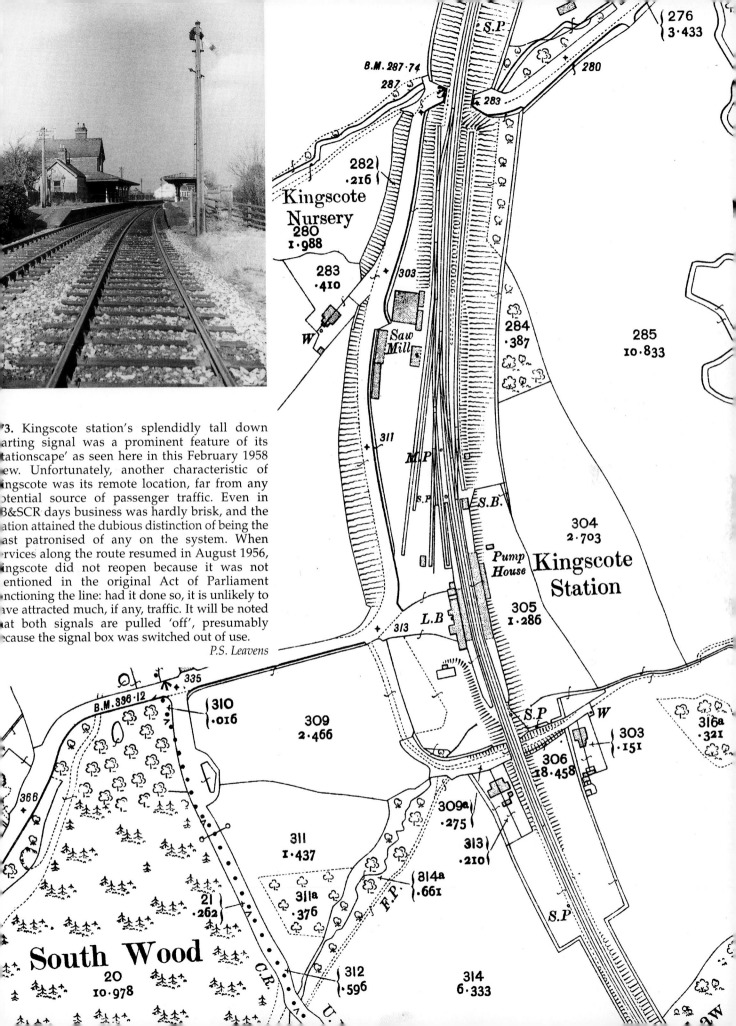

73. Kingscote station's splendidly tall down starting signal was a prominent feature of its 'stationscape' as seen here in this February 1958 view. Unfortunately, another characteristic of Kingscote was its remote location, far from any potential source of passenger traffic. Even in LB&SCR days business was hardly brisk, and the station attained the dubious distinction of being the least patronised of any on the system. When services along the route resumed in August 1956, Kingscote did not reopen because it was not mentioned in the original Act of Parliament sanctioning the line: had it done so, it is unlikely to have attracted much, if any, traffic. It will be noted that both signals are pulled 'off', presumably because the signal box was switched out of use.

P.S. Leavens

174. On a bright spring day, 16th April 1955, an Ivatt 2-6-2T, No. 41318, leaves Kingscote in charge of the 2.34pm Oxted to Lewes train, which is formed of a 'Birdcage' set of coaches.

J.J. Smith

175. The wooded slopes in the background of the previous photograph are now totally concealed by foliage, and even Kingscote station is only just visible through the gap in the trees in this picture taken on 9th October 1994. The elegant SE&CR H Class 0-4-4T No. 263 is seen running round its train prior to returning to Sheffield Park.

J.G. Mallinson

76. In superb evening light, Fairburn 2-6-4T locomotive No. 42086 wheels the 4.20pm London Bridge to Brighton train round the curve into Kingscote station on 31st August 1954. This locomotive was one of a batch of forty-one members of its type built at Brighton Works between July 1950 and June 1951, this particular example being constructed in March 1951. It remained in service until March 1967. *J.H. Aston*

Kingscote was described in an 1887 guide book as 'a railway station without a village', a description which remains valid to the present day. The early history of the station revolves around the personality of Thomas Ward who was the stationmaster at Kingscote until 1906. It is likely that the many stories about this gentleman have been exaggerated over the years, but even so it appears that he was quite a formidable character. He strove to make his station the smartest on the LB&SCR system, it being noted for the masses of roses which clustered around the platform fences. Best of all were the climbing roses which clung to canopy stanchions and dangled precariously from the canopies, and the baskets which hung from every available position. Mr. Ward was also a very religious man who held open-air meetings in the station forecourt if fine, or on the down-side platform when wet. The remote location of the station is perhaps best illustrated by quoting a former resident of Kingscote, Mr. A.H. Rowland, who stated that 'it was still remote when I was there in 1901/2, and approached from the west by a road deep in sand, through woods thick with primroses, and only a farm and market garden nearby'.

The station buildings at Kingscote were built in the same style as the others on the line, the main building being situated on the up side. The goods yard consisted of three sidings, two of which served the cattle dock and a large sawmill. The signal box was located at the north end of the down platform. Originally the station boasted fully canopied platforms but the facilities at Kingscote were, unfortunately, rationalised between the wars, in common with other stations on the line. The most noticeable result of this policy was the demolition of the down-side platform buildings and canopy, and their replacement with the 1930s equivalent of a bus stop shelter.

Little information about day-to-day life at the station has survived, but at least a few snippets have been passed down concerning the staff at Kingscote station in the period between the wars. The station had lost its independent status by 1925, coming under the jurisdiction of the stationmaster at East Grinstead. At this time the station staff apparently consisted of a team of three men, a booking clerk and two porter-signalmen who worked shifts. The duties of the latter included tending the oil lamps (there was no gas or electricity), assisting in the goods yard or operating a pump from which the water supplies were obtained.

Passenger traffic was never heavy, as might be expected at a station in such a rural location, and many of the regular passengers resided at scattered farms and large houses in the locality. The busiest train of the day was the 8.0am to Lewes, which conveyed passengers who travelled daily to Brighton. Cheap day tickets to South Coast resorts also produced a reasonable income, and Sunday excursion tickets to sporting events etc. were generally in demand. The station's relatively prosperous days prior to the Second World War were, however, never repeated. During the inter-war period goods traffic was also healthy, with Kingscote being the transfer point between two goods trains – one from Haywards Heath, and another from East Grinstead – which met there daily. There was a lot of timber traffic consisting of uncut treetrunks coming in and partly prepared timber being despatched. Milk, of course, was a major source of revenue, while incoming consignments of coal, manure and bricks produced five or six wagonloads a day. Occasionally there would be a special trainload of racehorses going to Ireland via Holyhead and returning by the same route.

continued overleaf

77. Rebirth of a railway! This was the scene at Kingscote in early 1994 when track-laying was in full swing and the finishing touches were being made to the station prior to reopening in April of that year. The large building on the left of the picture, which was formerly a sawmill, and the up platform, appear to have survived more or less intact, but there is little else to link the two photographs. The 'building' behind the fence on the right of the picture is part of the former Brighton Upper Goods signal box which will eventually be re-erected at Kingscote near the site of the original signal box. The section of the up platform with wooden paling fencing has been added by the Bluebell to enable it to accommodate seven-coach trains. The down platform has been completely rebuilt, hence the new brickwork.

J.G. Mallinson

178. A general view of Kingscote station from the north west with part of the goods yard on the right. The station's rural isolation is apparent, there being not a single dwelling in sight, apart from a glimpse of one of the railway cottages beyond the up platform buildings. Note the milepost which indicates that the station is fifteen miles from Culver Junction. This scene was photographed on 27th May 1955. *D. Cullum*

continued from previous page After the end of hostilities in 1945 there was a rapid decline in the fortunes of Kingscote, passenger traffic was down to a trickle and on the freight side a similar drastic reduction was evident. All small loads were distributed from East Grinstead and only wagonloads sent through which by this time consisted almost solely of shipments of timber. The signalbox was reduced to the status of a shunting cabin, being normally 'switched out', and the station staff consisted of one leading porter who undertook the varied duties of signalman, porter and booking clerk. Kingscote did not re-open in 1956 because it was not mentioned in the original Act of Parliament authorising the line, but remained intact for some years following closure. The goods yard was given a new lease of life as a refuge for condemned wagons, while even after the final closure the route remained open on a 'care and maintenance' basis. A visit in September 1961 revealed that roses were still thriving in the flower beds, a bit bedraggled perhaps, but still blooming despite years of neglect. The end for Kingscote came in 1965 when the demolition men moved in to remove the track, but the station buildings mercifully survived. Interestingly, Kingscote was the only station on the Lewes to East Grinstead line to retain its nameboards, which were still *in situ* when the line was being lifted! The painstaking restoration of Kingscote station in recent years is the latest chapter in its history, but that is another story.

179. The reopening of Kingscote station in April 1994, was a major milestone on the way towards Bluebell's long-term aim of restoring the line through to East Grinstead. Most of the painstaking restoration work on the main station building has been completed, but much other work remains outstanding, as is clearly apparent from the untidy state of the goods yard area, seen here on 15th February 1995. It is unlikely that the modern rail tank wagon, which contains an emergency locomotive water supply, and clearly looks out of place, will be part of the scene at Kingscote for long!
John Goss

80. The 3.28pm Haywards Heath to London Bridge train later formed a rush-hour return working for homegoing commuters and ʋas consequently a heavy formation, usually comprising six or seven vehicles of a variety of types. It is seen here leaving Kingscote ɩn 28th March 1955 with a set of Maunsell coaches in carmine and cream livery immediately behind the locomotive, Class N Mogul' No. 31823, which was also of Maunsell design. A total of eighty of these locomotives was built, at Ashford and Woolwich Arsenal, following the end of the First World War. They were versatile machines and worked in many areas of the Southern system, large number being based in the West Country for working the routes west of Exeter. Note the goods yard contains a wagon ɔaded with timber; also it appears to be washing day at the station house! *P. Hay*

181. During the autumn of 1958 race specials ran from Brighton to Lingfield: it is understood that special trains were provided for two 3-day meetings. In this extremely rare photograph of one of these unusual workings a SE&CR Class L 4-4-0 No. 31778 is seen using the down line in the up direction on 14th November. By this time the up line was out of use for running purposes and was, in effect, a siding used for the storage of withdrawn freight rolling stock. The down line, however, was not converted to a single line. Consequently, before a train could travel from Horsted Keynes to East Grinstead it was necessary to institute single line working by pilotman over the down line; this working ceased after the passage of the last (probably the only) up train on each occasion. The status of the down line was never altered; the occasional train in the down direction – such as an early morning newspaper train diverted from the main line due to engineering work – required no special arrangements. The train was photographed near Hazelden Farm, just as the sun was breaking through the morning mist.

J.C. Becket

2. An unidentified down train ambles along behind Ivatt 2-6-2T No. 41299 on 9th April 1955. This location is also adjacent to ⌐azelden Farm, which is just under a mile north of Kingscote station. The Turners Hill to East Grinstead road lies behind the trees ⌐ the right, while a hedgerow borders Imberhorne Lane in the top left hand corner of the picture. No. 41299 was built in November ⌐51 and survived until October 1966. Almost inevitably, a SE&CR three-coach 'Birdcage' set forms the train. Except for a small ⌐ction used by a local farmer as a track, the course of the line at this point has become very overgrown.   *N.W. Sprinks*

Imberhorne Cutting

183. Imberhorne Lane bridge provides a lofty vantage point for this photograph of the 2.59pm East Grinstead to Lewes train. The motive power is Ivatt Class 2MT 2-6-2T No. 41313 and this view was recorded on 27th May 1955. No. 41313 survived the scrapman's torch, and is today preserved at the Buckinghamshire Railway Centre.

D. Cullum

84. Class C2X 0-6-0 No. 32442 passes beneath Imberhorne Lane bridge, which carries a minor road across the railway. This location marks ~~he~~ the end of a mile-long 1 in 75 climb from Kingscote station, the remainder of the route into East Grinstead being level. The single coach ~~orming~~ forming the train is No. S3847S, an interesting LB&SCR vehicle with an aisle along one side; it was formerly used on the Midhurst branch. ~~his~~ This carriage formed many of the trains during the period of 'sulky service' running and later became a candidate for preservation by the ~~luebell~~ Bluebell. Sadly, when the coach was condemned it was quickly despatched to Newhaven for dismantling and broken-up before the Bluebell ~~uthorities~~ authorities were informed of its whereabouts. The train is the 11.30am *ex*-Lewes, and this portrait was recorded on 21st March 1957. *C. Hogg*

85. The final stage of the Bluebell Railway's plan to reopen the former ~~ine~~ line throughout to East Grinstead looks destined to be the most ~~omplex~~ complex and challenging so far. The most formidable obstacle is the ~~ormer~~ former cutting at Imberhorne which is seen in the two previous ~~lustrations~~ illustrations. Following the closure of the railway it was used as a tip, ~~nd~~ and has been infilled to within a few feet of the bridge parapets. Over ~~he~~ the years trees have become established on the surface of the tip and ~~notorists~~ motorists driving along Imberhorne Lane are probably unaware that ~~hey~~ they are crossing a bridge over a former railway. The magnitude of the ~~ask~~ task facing the Bluebell authorities can be gauged by comparing the ~~wo~~ two pictures. This picture of the scene, looking north from the bridge, ~~vas~~ was taken on 4th December 1994. The Bluebell will need a lot of luck – ~~ot~~ not to mention money – if their ambitious scheme is to succeed.

John Goss

186. Making a rare appearance on the line is a SE&CR C Class 0-6-0, No. 31724, seen here about a mile south of East Grinstead station with the 10.28am to Lewes on 21st March 1957. Note the milepost just to the left of the locomotive which indicates a distance of sixteen and a half miles from Culver Junction. The parapet of Imberhorne viaduct is just visible near the trees on the extreme right of the picture. The C Class was introduced in 1900, and subsequently 109 were built for freight duties. The sole survivor is preserved at the Bluebell Railway.

C. Hogg

187. During the early days of the Bluebell Railway a number of special trains were organised by the Bluebell Railway Preservation Society. The first of these ran on 12th July 1959 from Tonbridge to Lewes via East Grinstead (where the train gained access from the High Level to the Low Level via the 'goods spur) and Haywards Heath. The train returned via Uckfield. The Society's attempts to publicise the train were frustrated by a strike in the printing industry, but despite this problem the special was fully booked and many prospective passengers were disappointed. On arrival at Horsted Keynes the participants were addressed by the (then) Chairman of the BRPS, who spoke from a signal gantry about the Society's plans. The train is seen crossing Imberhorne viaduct on the outward journey powered by C2X Class 0-6-0 No. 32535, which was in pristine condition following an overhaul at Ashford Works. The BR Mk 1 coach formed immediately behind the locomotive had been added to the formation at Tunbridge Wells West and conveyed a private party. *J.C. Beckett*

Imberhorne Viaduct

188. The southern end of Imberhorne viaduct, seen here in February 1995, has an air of decay and neglect, an impression emphasised by the loss of many coping bricks which have been mindlessly removed by vandals. Brambles and saplings are starting to take hold, and are almost obscuring the southbound track at one point. Despite the misleading superficial appearance of the viaduct in this photograph it is still in basically sound condition. In September 1992 the Bluebell Railway purchased it from BR for a nominal sum, and are proceeding with a programme of minor repair work. *John Goss*

189. There is still frost on some of the sleepers as C2X Class No. 32521 comes off Imberhorne viaduct and approaches East Grinstead with a train from Lewes in December 1957.
P. Ha

190. The neat and well-ordered section of railway which used to operate at this point has been replaced by rusty and overgrown tracks, a wire mesh fence and mature trees. The viaduct parapet is visible in the middle of the picture. For many years the tracks on the viaduct were used to berth rolling stock at weekends, hence their retention long after the rest of the Horsted Keynes route was lifted. Both tracks are still *in situ* at the time of writing, but disused. The track behind the fence is electrified so presumably is used occasionally by the electric trains which now work the BR service from East Grinstead. *John Goss*

191. On 13th November 1954 C2X Class No. 32539 makes a spirited departure from East Grinstead with the 12.28pm football excursion to Lewes. The train comprises of Maunsell 3-set No. 962.   *C. Hogg*

192. Looking north from the same position today it is difficult to believe it is the same location. Hall & Co.'s 'Building Supplies Centre' now occupies a small area behind the trees on the right, but most of the former goods yard is now the site of a huge Sainsbury's supermarket, part of which is visible. The van in the foreground is owned by the Bluebell and temporarily based at East Grinstead in connection with the extension scheme. The town's skyline is now dominated by a massive multi-storey car park. Perhaps, if all the town's rail links had survived, such a monstrosity would not have been needed.   *John Goss*

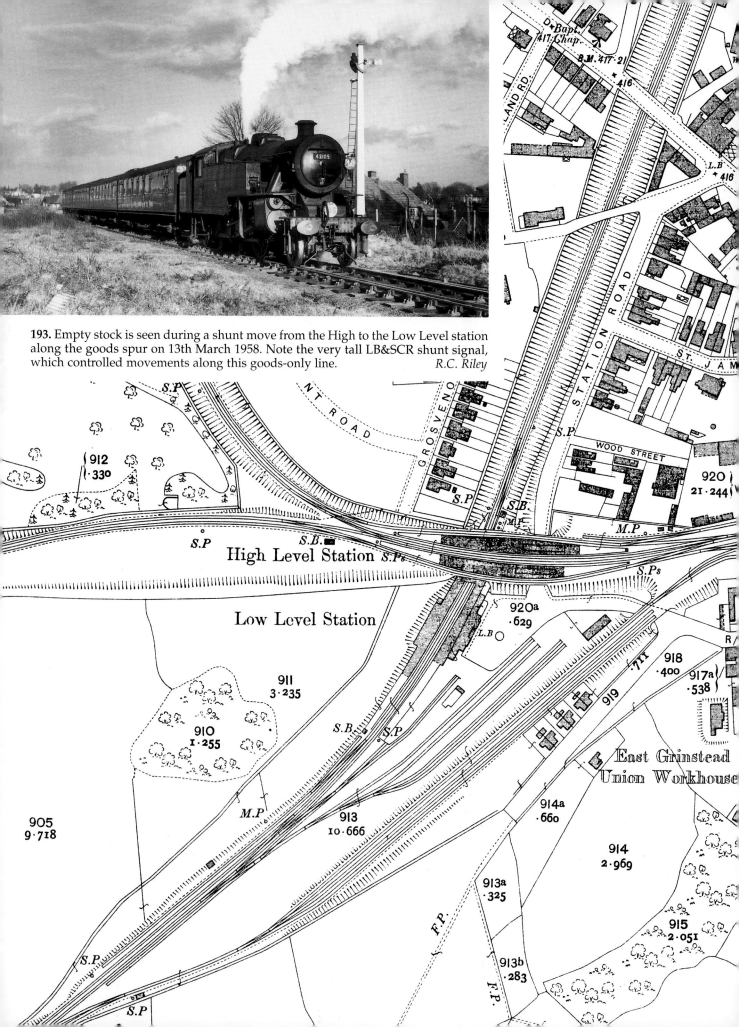

193. Empty stock is seen during a shunt move from the High to the Low Level station along the goods spur on 13th March 1958. Note the very tall LB&SCR shunt signal, which controlled movements along this goods-only line. *R.C. Riley*

High Level Station

Low Level Station

East Grinstead
Union Workhouse

194. The 3.30pm from Lewes, with C2X Class No. 32442 in charge, is about to pass the delightful timber signal box at East Grinstead on 2nd September 1956.

N.W. Sprinks

East Grinstead

195. The infrastructure at East Grinstead Low Level has been considerably rationalised over the years in order to reduce costs, and surplus railway land sold off for development. On the left of the picture the Messrs. Hall & Co.'s 'Building Supplies Centre' is visible in the background. The up and down running lines now merge into a headshunt which extends almost as far as the viaduct. The most obvious casualty of the rationalisation is the signal box which was replaced by the new computerised Oxted power signal box on 18th July 1987, a few months before the introduction of electric working. The Bluebell Railway acquired the fifteen-lever arrangement Saxby and Farmer frame for future use on the Northern Extension, so at least part of the signal box will live on!

J.G. Mallinson

196. In this view, taken in LB&SCR days, a D3 Class 0-4-4T No. 380 waits in the down platform before departing with the 7.7pm to Lewes. The train, which had previously formed the 5.5pm Victoria to East Grinstead, is formed of vintage six-wheel carriages. No. 380, formerly named *Thornton Heath*, was built in July 1893 and accumulated more than one and a half million miles in service before withdrawal in April 1953. It was amongst the last survivors of its class. Unfortunately the precise date of this photograph is unknown.   *Bluebell Archives*

197. Standing in a similar position to the train in the previous photograph is this one-coach working to Lewes which was photographed in June 1957, during the era of the so-called 'sulky service'. The station buildings do not appear to have changed greatly during the intervening period. The train is headed by an E4 Class 0-6-2T 'Large Radial', a type first introduced in December 1897. No. 32494 was built in November 1899 at Brighton Works and originally named *Woodgate*; it was withdrawn from service in September 1959.   *R. Hobbs*

198. The magnificent LB&SCR station building was, sadly, demolished in the early 1970s and replaced by a functional prefabricated building. The wooden paling fence on the right of the picture appears to be the only feature of the old station which has survived, apart from the platforms themselves. Beyond the station, huge buildings out of all proportion to those in the rest of the town now dominate the skyline. Such is progress! This scene was recorded on 15th February 1995. *John Goss*

199. In this charming picture, LB&SCR E4 Class No. 32475 is seen waiting to leave East Grinstead with the 12.28pm football special t
Lewes on 28th November 1953. The locomotive bears a '75A' shedplate, indicating that it is based at Brighton shed, a depot whic
was noted for the cleanliness of its engines, as exemplified here by the highly polished condition of No. 32475. The locomotive's crew
have already ensured it has sufficient steam raised to start the journey – at least judging by the steam escaping through the safet
valves – and have found time to chat to a gentleman on the platform. It is possible, of course, that he is a soccer fan *en route* to Brighto
to watch 'The Albion', but more likely a railway enthusiast, perhaps requesting an unofficial footplate ride!

C. Hog

200. The 4.8pm (or 16.08hrs. in 24-hour clock parlance!) train t
Victoria leaves East Grinstead on 15th February 1995. Compared t
the old days when the 'double decker' station was still in operation
it must be said that this scene is totally soulless, uninspiring and
a!most completely devoid of railway atmosphere. The train servic
to London is however the best the town has ever enjoyed. Perhaps
one day, if the Bluebell Railway's current extension plans materialise
some of that long-forgotten 'railway atmosphere' may return.

John Gos

201. SE&CR C Class 0-6-0 No. 31725 stands at East Grinstead station's low level up platform after arriving with a one coach train from Lewes in June 1957. An E4 Class 0-6-2T can just be seen in the background backing on to the train bunker-first before performing the shunting move to the down platform. *R. Hobbs*

202. A member of BR staff adjusts the headboard on BR Standard Class 4MT 2-6-4T No. 80154 prior to its shunt across to the down platform where a large crowd is waiting to board the last train to Lewes on 16th March 1958. *Mike Esau*

The friendly enginemen on the footplate of C2X Class 0-6-0 No. 32536 lean from the cab to greet the photographer as their steed climbs the stiff 1 in 80 incline away from Culver Junction, on the sunny autumn afternoon of 27th October 1956. The classic combination of a C2X Class locomotive and LB&SCR coach was a familiar sight on the Bluebell line in its last years, so it is an appropriate choice for the final illustration in this album. It is a tragedy that an example of this class of engine, and type of coach, was not preserved for posterity. Perhaps one day a generous benefactor may sponsor the construction of a C2X Class from scratch – who knows?

J.H.W. Kent

Acknowledgement

Preparation of a volume such as this is dependent upon the goodwill of a large number of people and I, therefore, willingly acknowledge the kind assistance provided by so many people, some of whom I have never met. Firstly, I would like to thank Chris Evans, David J. Fakes, Graham Mallinson and John J. Smith who scrutinized my original manuscript, and made many constructive criticisms and comments, which I feel have greatly improved the finished product. Simon Baker, Peter Thomas, Roger Williams and Charles Vigor also provided help with the manuscript. The success of an album of this type is dependent upon the quality of the original prints used for illustrations, and most have been printed by Derek Mercer whose expertise in this area has been invaluable. I must not forget Sue Wilkie who made an excellent job of typing the manuscript. The staff at the East Sussex Record Office, Lewes, have been unfailingly helpful when dealing with my various requests. Stephen Mourton, proprietor of Runpast Publishing, has once again given me total freedom to select the pictures and undertake my own design work. A special 'thank you' is due to John Goss and Graham Mallinson who have taken almost all the contemporary photographs. Both gentlemen are skilful and highly artistic photographers who have produced pictures of the highest quality. The following is a list of photographers who submitted historical material for publication to whom I also offer my grateful thanks: J.H. Aston, R. Bamberough, John Beckett, David Clark, David Cross, D. Cullum, Gerald Daniels, John Edgington, Mike Esau, John Faulkner, J. Spencer Gilks, Peter Hay, Roy Hobbs, Colin Hogg, P.J. Kelly, J.H.W. Kent, Paul Leavens, Phil Lynch, R.F. Roberts, D. Trevor Rowe, John Scrace, Gerald Siviour, John J. Smith, John L. Smith, W.A.C. Smith, N.W. Sprinks and Edwin Wilmshurst. Lastly, I would never forgive myself if I omitted to acknowledge the endless patience and understanding displayed by my wife, Christine, during the compilation of this book.

Bibliography

Most of the historical information used in this album has been previously published in *Bluebell News*, journal of the Bluebell Railway Preservation Society, and is reproduced here with the kind permission of the former editor, Klaus Marx. In addition to *Bluebell News*, I have also referred to the excellent series of locomotive histories produced by the Railway Correspondence and Travel Society, and to the *Railway Magazine*.